Without Warning

JANE O'CONNOR

Without Warning

One woman's story
of surviving Black Saturday

hardie grant books
MELBOURNE · LONDON

Published in 2010 by
Hardie Grant Books
85 High Street
Prahran, Victoria 3181, Australia
www.hardiegrant.com.au

Cataloguing-in-Publication data is available from the National Library of Australia.
Without Warning: One woman's story of surviving Black Saturday
ISBN 978 1 74066 847 7

Cover design by Christabella Designs
Front cover image courtesy of Newspix/Alex Coppel
Back cover image courtesy of RSPCA/James Walshe Photography
Text design and typesetting by Cannon Typesetting
Typeset in Garamond 12/20 pt
Printed and bound in Australia by McPherson's Printing Group

10 9 8 7 6 5 4 3 2 1

For Sean and my resilient family

'When I count my blessings, I count you twice'—Irish proverb

Contents

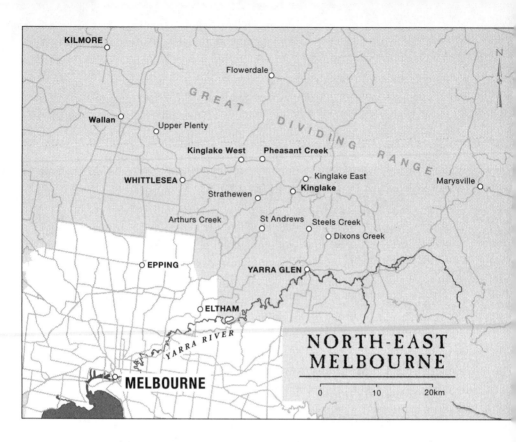

NORTH-EAST MELBOURNE

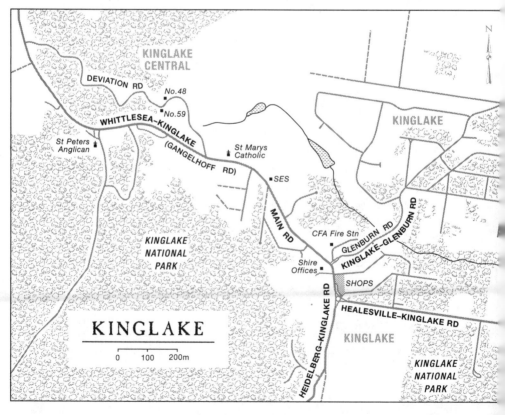

KINGLAKE

Prologue

I'M trying to follow the voice that is screaming my name, getting closer and closer now but still barely audible over the noise. I have no idea how long I've been trapped here in the study, watching the monstrous force outside devour everything in its path. It's toppling massive trees, and flinging balls of burning gas like missiles; I can see the air burning.

Is it going to tear the roof off, blast out the windows? Or maybe it will barrel in under the verandah and set the house on fire? Is there any way I can get outside and onto some navigable, already burnt ground? Above all, I must try to keep breathing, despite the dense, acrid smoke. I've already watched the heat melt my car in the driveway. There's no exit that way.

The voice breaks through the racket again: 'Jane, Jane, where are you?' It's Sean. I yell back that I'm up the front of the house. 'Get down to the back, I'm outside the laundry,' I hear. How he can bear the heat out there, let alone breathe, I can't imagine. I inch down the hallway—moving fast is too big an assault on my lungs and eyes, and I'm already feeling lightheaded from inhaling so much smoke. Every window I pass frames an unimaginable inferno.

I get to the kitchen and almost sink to my knees; it's as if a pair of hands is crushing my lungs. The air is like liquid plastic, coating my mouth, nose and eyes. Keep breathing, just keep breathing, I tell myself, though overwhelmingly I feel I might black out at any moment. But I have to fight it, not give in; the back door is only metres away. I make it to the laundry door—I'm gasping, can't see properly, but I've come this far, I'm not going to give up now.

PART I

Mountain refuge

1

Mountain life

Our spot in the Kinglake Ranges outside Melbourne has always been a cooler, green haven in summer. In fact it's a bit of a misnomer to call this a mountain range, as it's not much more than 600 metres above sea level at the highest point. But it isn't hard to see why generations before us have sloughed off the city heat and grit, and headed for higher, lusher pastures when lowland temperatures go for that long, slow, brown summer bake.

There are remnants of that quest for summer respite. Quaint weatherboard and fibro guesthouses dating back to the 1920s and 1930s nestle among giant tree ferns and eucalypts on ridges and in gullies. More the preserve of the wealthy—those who could afford the car needed to make the journey less arduous. Not hard to imagine them lumbering up the steep, rough track, hoping the radiator didn't boil; it wasn't a day trip then. But it was a popular destination for honeymooners and picnickers who came to marvel at the forests, fern gullies and waterfalls of the 22 360-hectare national park. Those early buildings were supplemented over the years with less salubrious weekend cottages, converted sheds and camping spots that echoed with the laughter of schoolchildren on holiday while the adults fanned themselves under the spreading European trees that thrive in the deep mountain loam. Breeze catchers, shade givers. The park, created in 1928 to stop the rampant clearing of land for farming, is only around 65 kilometres north-east of Melbourne, an accessible day trip these days.

It has often entered my head, while pushing some zippy little car up the final 13-kilometre stretch of winding road between St Andrews and Kinglake (known to the locals as 'the Windies'), what extraordinary feats the first farmers and settlers here must have achieved, reliant as they were on horses and buggies to get them through the rocky, precipitous bush. Nothing sealed and bump-free in those days. However, the lure of gold was a strong incentive and long-abandoned shafts can still be found in parts of the national park and on private land. It remains a narrow road, chipped out of bedrock; native fauna in search of roadside green pickings or water bound or scurry across your path without warning. These days, though, there are luminous white lines and large reflective arrows to chart your course.

It's easy to spot a first-time visitor or tourist on this road. The sheer drops off one side, tumbling down into the seemingly bottomless gullies of the national park, make drivers nervous and they crawl gingerly as close as possible to the middle white line; they have barely a brake lining left by the time they get to the top. Some locals never get used to it either, choosing to take more roundabout but less demanding routes. It is a dramatic landscape and perhaps the temptation to drink it in, coupled with very few spots to pull over and stop, compounds visitors' slowness. The lower-lying contoured farmlands give way to archetypal, parched struggling bush: the type of sparse, scrubby flora that has to punch its way up slowly from flinty bedrock, clinging tenaciously to the steeper folds and gullies. Topsoil is hard to find; the sounds of birds ping through this sort of bush. It's murder on a hot day, almost as though the rock reflects the heat and throws it back in your face. Crunchy and twig-snapping underfoot; the constant hum of insects.

Yet as you start to climb, once 'the Windies' are in sight, all thoughts of a sweaty workday in the urban jungle start to fall away: in ten minutes the familiar landscape of home will bring relief. Then, approaching the apex, there's a sense of relaxation. The horticultural strugglers on the southern side of the mountain cede territory to massive, ancient mountain ash trees—the world's tallest flowering plant—which tower over the roadway, their crowns reaching for the sky out of gully floors. The ferns change too: here they are tall enough to stand under, with succulent green fronds. Wind down the window and breathe in the damper, cooler air. Drive in under a huge green umbrella that filters the sun and gives life to denser, more diverse undergrowth.

At the top of the mountain road, the preserved green zone gives way to people and a built environment. Houses nestle in the bush or perch on ridge roads to capture stunning views that range from the city skyline to the beautiful contours of the wine-growing Yarra Valley. Kinglake township, with its service station and take-away pizza shop on the left, the stone café and supermarket and group of shops on the right. Straight ahead sits the Country Fire Authority (CFA) station and the National Park Hotel—the latter more than a century old, and refurbished over the years but still screaming of the 1960s.

Even from the township, the once-extensive farmlands are still evident. The deep, rich, red mountain soil has produced endless tonnes of potatoes, carrots, leafy green crops, luscious berries and chubby sheep. Once it became obvious that the gold lode wasn't as rich as expected, the settlers turned their attention to logging the eucalypts. But that started to slope off as early as the 1930s, to be superseded mainly by potato and berry farming. In the sixteen years my husband Sean and I have been here, the ploughed furrows, sweeping pastures and plentiful water have increasingly been given over to housing. The streets surrounding the town are now a suburb and new estates have sprung up as tired farmers have sought retirement and subdivided their land rather than persisting in the battle to sell produce in a monopolised market.

When we arrived, back then, jinkers loaded to the gunwales with long, straight timbers bound for the mills still regularly traversed the town. For me, the sound of their engine brakes roaring as they came down the main-road hill was a sad one, heralding an ignoble end for the fabulous trees ripped out of nearby coupes. Then, as anti-logging pressure mounted and industry prices dropped, the trees found their way into woodchip piles a long, long way from home.

Sean and I had long hankered after this quieter, cleaner, greener place. Logistics and work requirements saw us start our joint life in inner Melbourne—close to the city, with markets, restaurants, cafes and shops all within walking distance, but not our natural habitat. When we first contemplated moving to the distant hills, friends and colleagues thought we were barking mad to want to exchange a café latte on the doorstep for a very long commute to a place most of them hadn't heard of. Family and income needs made our relocation a gradual process: we inched further and further out until we found ourselves at the bottom of the mountain, looking up.

We took to heading up the windy road for, of all things, a parcel of freshly cooked fish and chips. Those sorties led to explorations of the roadways, backblocks and lookout points with a view to finding a property to buy. One Saturday afternoon we turned into Deviation Road, which loops off the main road that runs west from Kinglake towards Whittlesea. Originally the main road and then known as The Deviation, it meanders through a mixture of undulating paddocks and native bush before rejoining the Whittlesea–Kinglake Road.

As we rounded one of the bends, we saw a 'For Sale' sign tacked at the front of a property on the left-hand side, Number 59. We'd been watching the real-estate ads and had looked at another property on this road, rejecting it for its poor structural integrity and the residual dieldrin in the soil from potato-farming days when such toxic additives were the norm rather than the exception. At that time we'd noticed the nearby properties, including Number 59—an older-style, tin-roofed house that had been reskinned with Hardiplank and extended, with a verandah that ran across the front and down one side. An extensive cottage garden carpeted the understorey of soaring mountain ash. A sweeping lawn beside the house boasted a grand old sycamore tree; the front verge offered up the sort of massive ash that belonged in a colonial landscape painting—priceless trees that take decades to reach such noble proportions. A couple of cows were languidly grazing on a verdant paddock that rolled up one side of the property and around to the back boundary. The 'For Sale' sign was the kind that goes up before the agent has had the chance to produce a swankier board for the roadside.

'Looks like it needs a fair bit of work. There's not much to the fences,' Sean said. He went on to itemise water tanks in need of replacement, a roof that probably leaked, how many metres of fence would be needed, old sheds, and blackberry about as big, healthy and tenacious as a noxious weed gets.

'Look at the garden, though. It's a very pretty spot and it's got to be cheaper than the same sort of land area closer to town. It doesn't cost anything to ask,' I retorted.

We took the contact number and rang from the nearest phone. The agent, Alan O'Gorman, made an appointment to show us through straight away. He was a delight to deal with: no hard sell, just professional, honest and nice, and he knew the area and the property backwards. He drew particular attention to the quality of the deep artesian bore near the house, which had been installed many years ago. Kinglake has long been noted for its accessible groundwater, but the cost of sinking a bore can be considerable. To have one on the property already was a bonus. Less than a week later we'd bought ourselves a home, warts and all. We had no romantic illusions: it was going to be a bit of a slog, with no quick fixes—the O'Connors had acquired a work in progress.

We moved there in the middle of a Kinglake winter—howling gale, teeming rain, freezing temperatures. The vendor's bank had lost the title documents and scuttled the late-Friday settlement, so we sat in the driveway in despair as the solicitors worked out an after-hours deal, while two disgruntled furniture removalists griped about the time and sloshed through the mud with our worldly goods. Our cream lounge suite ended up in the mire and we faced a night with no gas or electricity. But it didn't matter.

Once the legalities were sorted out, the sleeves got rolled up. The unglamorous things begged for attention first: fences, new tanks, septic system, driveways, gutters, rubbish, animal shelters, overgrown garden, sheds, paint. Gumboots and Blundstones, oil-skins and beanies became the weekend uniform. But we took to it like ducks to water, as did our dogs—there have always been dogs. When we weren't digging, rebuilding or straining something, we could walk up the road uninterrupted or meander through the bush. The dogs would come too—roaring into wombat burrows, leaping into a stream or dam, running free, never chained up. An integral part of our entertainment was the birdlife: listening to lyrebirds going love-crazy after rain, counting the generations of kookaburras, laughing at mother magpies teaching babies to pull worms from a damp lawn, marvelling at the spinebills hovering for nectar from fuschias and Chinese lantern flowers.

After the first two or three years, we'd become familiar with the way the garden behaved and had renovated parts of it. A vegetable plot emerged and we took great delight in scoring a truckload of cheap Colorbond sheets to build 'Chookingham Palace' for the hens. On those working Sundays we became used to the sound of the CFA siren going off down in the township. It gave us a bit of a fright at first, but over time we came to know that it usually spelt the fire crews having a practice session. Unless the old red truck ground its way up the main-road hill, we didn't pay much attention, and even that often signalled some emergency other than a fire, such as a car accident. We often remarked on how long it took that veteran vehicle to grind its way to the top of the rise, straining in first gear.

The daunting tangle of blackberry gradually succumbed to the grubbing, chopping, burning and rotary-hoeing, with help from our pet goats. The native seeds that Sean's father Mick religiously collected on his long walks and propagated for us were planted as a grove that swept from the main road right through to the much-loved sycamore tree. After he died, we took comfort and pleasure in seeing 'Mickey's trees' grow like topsy in their new home.

As the budget allowed, we tackled the interior of the house. Apart from the kitchen and bathroom renovations, Sean did most of the work. It was a tour of discovery: wrenching out an old wall oven revealed an original chimney cavity, which we lined out to form a large cupboard; yanking up vinyl floor coverings brought to light Baltic-pine floorboards bearing the scars of old potato sacks. The sacks would be piled on the floor and stencilled, one by one, with the grower's name before being filled and sent to market. No amount of sanding removed the stencil ink and in fact we didn't want to.

Family and friends formed a constant flow of through-traffic at weekends. For some, the pull of the mountain was particularly strong. My niece Jo-Anna, who had left New Zealand for her first bit of travel, ended up staying with us for a year. Her brother Brad would hop across the Tasman for regular catch-ups too, or detour through on his way back from elsewhere. Jo would fill us with dread, hurtling down 'the Windies' on her racing road bike to a weekend job. The ride back up was tougher, especially in winter, but once past the last bend before home in Deviation Road she was greeted by the verandah lights shining through the mist: 'It's like Battlestar Galactica,' she'd say, 'guiding you in for a landing.' The name stuck. The Battlestar was a safe place to be.

While we worked on the property, the people in our orbit became an integral part of life: once on the mountain at weekends, there was little desire to travel long distances for entertainment. From housing a sparse population of permanent residents, the road gradually began to fill up. Hanging over a fence for a natter was normal, though in our neighbourhood it wasn't that cheek-by-jowl proximity that you find in more urban environments. The properties ranged in size from around 1 hectare up to 16.

As you head west out of Kinglake on the main road, Deviation Road branches off to the right. This lower end was defined by three smaller holdings with views out across fields and bush, and further on to the Great Dividing Range. At the beginning of this section were Lynne and Barry Southern, among the few permanent residents here when we arrived. A little further along was a small white cottage on around 13 hectares, which remained unoccupied until an elderly couple moved in as caretakers for a cattle-farming operation. The road meandered around bends, revealing homes and larger acreages, before beginning to climb towards more heavily treed properties in the middle section, where the dense foliage shrouded some houses from view. The point where the bitumen joins up again with the main road was defined by the pristine fields farmed by the extended Singh family, who worked day and night to turn a rabbit- and blackberry-infested wasteland into a productive vegetable farm.

Julie Hansen and her husband John Christadoulou had retired to their property, which stood diagonally across the road from Number 59, several years after we first moved in. John had built most of the house over six or seven years and Julie had engaged in a constant battle with the unforgiving north wind to establish a fabulous garden; it all looked out on a beautiful stand of bush and across green fields to those distant blue-hazed ranges. The four of us quickly settled into a natural, easy pattern of sharing a meal, chattering about building projects and garden ideas and, always, the weather. We would keep an eye on each other's properties if either couple was away.

The Chandlers, landlocked at the end of an easement running through John and Julie's property, were happy in their mudbrick house, farming sheep as a sideline and generating their own power and water. Their son Tim would head through our paddocks each morning, to cut a long round trip off his school bus ride, and stop for a chat. Later, when Tim went to university, that well-worn path was trodden by Kevin Smith, the eldest of three who had moved in next door with their parents Dionne and Mark. Their property, also at the lower end of Deviation Road, adjoins ours on two boundaries. It was heartening to see the generations ticking over and watch as Kevin replaced Tim in dodging our two nosy horses, Ricky and Eliza—acquired along the way—and an even nosier trio of white goats—the offspring and remnants of our original blackberry-eaters. Kevin's younger brother Kane and little sister Kelsey were also regular visitors and Kelsey would line up to stay the night when Dionne and Mark went out.

The Cahills owned a property further along the road, adjoining John and Julie's: they lived off the mountain, but would come up at weekends. Next to them were Karen Ostenried and husband Bernie Svoboda, who had moved to the road before us and did so owing in part to their love of horses. Once past their property, the left-hand side of the road—with bush blocks and ferny, shaded gullies—was sparsely populated. Towards the top end of the road stood Peter Mitchell's attractive mudbrick house with its views out through a stand of mountain ash. Here too were the Lawless family, Pam and Terry and their son Craig; Terry and Craig had a long history of service with the CFA. Kate and Ivan Rowbotham were building their retirement home at the far end of the road, where it rejoined the main road.

Others from further afield became friends when local issues spurred us into collective action, and of course people with similar interests and senses of humour tend naturally to gravitate towards each other. At the same time, nobody on the mountain intruded unnecessarily on anyone else; we all enjoyed our solitude and respected it in others. But we'd share surplus vegies, keep an eye on each other's properties, help if needed, swap notes about experiences and, out of necessity, observe the seasons coming and going.

The Chandlers kept detailed weather records for their sheep and horticultural production.

The seasons are very distinctive on the mountain. There is the obvious—drifts of bulbs pushing through in spring, bees coming out of hibernation, the rate at which the pasture grows, vegie and fruit harvests, autumn leaves, snow most winters. Acutely aware of bird and animal behaviour and bush signals, Sean has always had an extra sense, what he calls 'a gypsy instinct', about what may or may not be on the weather horizon. He is also a natural conversationalist and could often be found engaging the brain of one of the older farmers or residents he'd run into.

A normal part of the seasonal routine was the annual burn-off. All jokes about men and boxes of matches aside, it was a long-standing ritual in late autumn or early spring to clear as much undergrowth and combustible debris as possible. There was only a small window of opportunity to get the piles dry enough before burn-off restrictions came into force. Summer rain was the norm on the mountain—grass up to the fence tops before you knew it, high hay yields, well-fed livestock. When the lowland world was getting browned off, we'd crow about still being green. Sean's brother Marty would drive up from the flatlands of the baking northern suburbs and declare, 'It's like a different world up here.'

We were able at times to offer farmers elsewhere, in the grip of severe drought, the use of our lush land to save a core herd.

Over the years the burn-off morphed into a social occasion. At some point, the council contractors stopped slashing the growth along the roadside. (As we'd planted our own verges, we weren't in fact sorry to see the last of the mower that charged indiscriminately through our handiwork.) We all picked up the slack, mowing as well as clearing bark and fallen tree limbs. The ensuing burn-off was a Sunday job, with lots of conversation about fire behaviour, the odd flame that escaped and needed reining in; in the late afternoon we'd all share a cold glass of wine and a plate of nibbles. Sean would keep tabs on the ember piles for the rest of the night and we'd feel satisfied that our fuel-reduction efforts were in order.

From 2004, though, the burnable mounds turned into huge piles. Summer rain dried up and the winters didn't bring their usual degree of bogging mud. The howling northerlies came belting in earlier, often before Christmas; the paddocks turned brown and crisp. We were burning off several times a season instead of just once, and the roadside heaps formed a string of beacon fires that must have looked eerie to airline pilots flying into Melbourne. It was a struggle to keep gardens watered as rainwater-tank contents dropped. Fruits and vegetables would ripen, whereas they'd struggled to get enough heat before. Our mountain climate was palpably changing.

The timber deck Sean and I had added to the side of the house became an observation post, the place to flop once you'd got up 'the Windies' on a hot day. Whatever Melbourne's thermometer says, you can shave around six degrees off that for the mountain: what the weather bureau predicts for the metropolis has to be recalibrated for Kinglake. Add the awning provided by the trees and we could feel smug when sweltering friends rang to bemoan the pitiless heat elsewhere; here, a day that brought 36°C was considered aberrant. Not for us too many nights of pacing the floor, too hot to sleep—we'd just head for the deck, or for the backyard now beautifully paved with old factory bricks. A glass of wine in hand, we'd kick back and watch the summer world instead of television. The dogs—black labrador Harley, blue-heeler-cross Meg, and Jazz the Jack Russell cross—sprawled at our feet or hung over the end of the verandah.

Early evening was peak-hour for birds, which chattered in and out of the towering mountain ash until dusk put them to sleep. Parrots came in for seed and for water that was always topped up and cool. Stunning green and orange king parrots became bold enough to tap on the window—ominous, given they normally prefer to be at lower altitudes and around water. We were also being visited by larger kangaroos rather than the smaller wallabies we were used to; they were getting higher and higher up the mountain in their search for food and drink. Butterflies formed a colourful, fluttering cloud in the flowering gum, while the speckled brown birds known as tree creepers vacuumed bugs from its bark. 'It's amazing how much life there is in that one tree,' Sean often observed. We'd watch the sun set and turn the wattles from purple to blue–grey, the thick clouds of insects just above the paddock grass, and the swallows zeroing in for a feeding frenzy (this swooping, bug-eating activity always happened between weather fronts). Sean would rail at the flocking Indian myna birds that invaded his line of sight. 'Bloody cane toads with wings,' he'd mutter. Like cane toads in northern Queensland, Indian mynas were imported to control crop pests but became pests themselves: Sean had declared war on them for invading the nesting sites of native birds.

The deck was the venue for many a conversation about fire-safety planning too. The devastating bushfires that had ripped through the state of Victoria in January 1939 were still talked about. It was the state's worst fire tragedy, known henceforth as Black Friday: seventy people died and two million hectares of land, plus entire townships, were destroyed; the old-timers around Kinglake still talked about it. A long, severe drought saw uncontrolled smaller fires that had been burning for a week turn into giant, rampaging firestorms as temperatures soared and winds whipped up to the extent that flames were leaping from mountain peak to mountain peak. The massive fireballs that threatened or wiped out townships were etched forever into the memories of survivors. In those days firefighting brigades, which received little financial support from the government, used wet hessian sacks as their primary weapon.

The forests of the Great Dividing Range were devastated by one of the first fire outbreaks—at Toolangi, near Kinglake—in early January that year. Attempts to contain it failed and the flames burnt into the Lower Acheron Valley and Narbethong before racing through the Cathedral Range near Buxton and on towards Marysville. Outbreaks ringed towns such as Warburton before wind changes saved them. Others were not so lucky, with small forest towns such as Noojee being wiped out and dozens of sawmills and properties destroyed in iconic locations such as Bright. A deliberately lit fire near Colac in the Western District leapt through the hills to the seaside retreat of Lorne, sending people scurrying onto the beach for safety. Warrandyte, on Melbourne's outer-eastern fringe, was also threatened and the Black Forest near Woodend in the Macedon Ranges was all but destroyed. The subsequent royal commission's findings laid the basis for much of today's bushfire policy and led to the establishment, in 1945, of a single rural firefighting agency, the Country Fire Authority.

While Kinglake township largely escaped the full onslaught of Black Friday, the ranges surrounding it lay in ruins. The destructive Ash Wednesday fires of 16 February 1983 also spared the town, but the resulting development of a 'Stay and defend or go early' policy was well known, well studied and well discussed. Ash Wednesday was tattooed on my brain; I was working at the time as Victorian news editor for the national wire service, Australian Associated Press. On 16 February, the newsroom went onto full alert as the world watched a series of smaller fires picked up by a violent wind change and racing, in one day, through the Dandenong Ranges near Melbourne, wiping out most of Mount Macedon and roaring down the Great Ocean Road to burn out communities such as Aireys Inlet and Anglesea before again being stopped by the ocean at Lorne. In Victoria, there were forty-seven dead; in South Australia, the death toll was twenty-eight. Around 8000 people were evacuated and the loss of homes and buildings was horrendous. I still recall clearly the reports of giant fireballs, formed by eucalyptus gas, being flung kilometres ahead of fire fronts, and the descriptions of the jet-like roar as fronts approached.

The 'Stay and defend or go early' policy, which began to be developed after Ash Wednesday but was not fully introduced for several years, was unique to Australia. It was based on findings from previous deadly bushfires that people who could stay and defend their property—sheltering in the house until a firestorm passed and then actively attacking any ember strikes—had a higher chance of survival than those who fled late and were trapped on roads. There was an understanding between us Deviation Road residents about who would stay and who would go in the event of a bushfire.

By the beginning of 2006 we were noticing that there was an increasing number of total-fire-ban days. The radio was automatically tuned to the ABC (the state's emergency broadcaster) throughout summer, and we developed our own fire plans. These were tested on Australia Day that year, when a blaze broke out near Kinglake, its front clearly visible from Deviation Road.

As soon as the alert went out we made the firm decision to stay, as did John and Julie, the Chandlers and the Cahills. We had organised the safety clothing, worked out what to do in the event of an ember attack, and formed a united neighbourhood front to keep each other informed of any falling, burning debris. It was clearly understood that the behaviour of the wind would be crucial. We blocked up doors and windows with wet towels and constantly soaked walls, gutters, roofs, verandahs and any combustible material. A convoy of horse floats and livestock trucks headed past our back boundary, taking animals to safety at council facilities that had been set up in Whittlesea. As soon as the fire was observed, emergency services had arrived on the scene and we felt fully prepared to stay and defend our own patch, and even to lend the neighbours a hand if necessary. The Smiths were in Perth with Kevin, while Dionne's father minded the other two children at home. The couple next to John and Julie also planned to stay, despite being in their eighties, as they weren't willing to leave the cattle behind. Most of the residents at the top, heavily treed end of the road—including the Lawless family, with all their firefighting knowledge—had said that in the event of a major outbreak they would most likely head off the mountain, judging their properties too hard to defend.

Our road became a vantage point for local fire crews who had been assigned to the township to respond to building fires and to protect as many homes as possible in the local area they were familiar with. Aggravating 'rubber-neckers' arrived in droves too, dumping their rubbish, sitting on their car roofs as if they were at a country football match, and generally getting underfoot until the police cleared them out. The wind was dancing in all directions, taking the fire front first one way and then another. We followed the emergency services broadcasts like they were the bible and trusted our own eyes, ears and instincts. We donned our fire clothing—overalls, boots, woollen shirts, masks, hats, gloves, goggles—and there was a tacit understanding that we wouldn't be getting any sleep until it was over. There was time to prepare fire-breaks, rake up more flammable material, fill gutters with water, drench garden beds and external structures, fill extra water receptacles and place them strategically around the house, top up water tanks from the artesian bore, prepare food in case of power cuts. We worked calmly in unison in the way we'd planned, dealing efficiently with falling embers and checking on others to see if they needed help. As the wind brought burning gum leaves and twigs onto the property, we would either hose them out or attack them with wet towels or a soaking mop. Walking around the exterior of the house constantly, watching for any points where embers might enter, became our constant patrol. If embers did fall, we'd call John and Julie to ensure that they too were on the lookout.

The fire crews watching from the roadside described this as a 'lazy' fire, as distinct from those whipped to a frenzy by ferocious wind and heat. By now, most of the women and children had left the mountain. As one of the few women left, and the holder of an advanced food-handling qualification, I joined the pub's landlady, Michelle Dunscombe, and—with new crews still rolling in from across and outside the state—we pumped out up to 600 meals a night for hungry firefighters, with help from anyone we could dragoon into action. Supplying food for crews was a matter of controversy at the time: bureaucracy had gone mad over the issue of food hygiene and safety, with the result that the activities of traditional Australian providers of fire-front fodder, such as the Country Women's Association, Salvation Army and Red Cross, had been put on hold. But we had a commercial kitchen, a trained food-handler and an army of exhausted firefighters lining up—there was no way they weren't going to get a decent meal.

The ABC broadcasts belted out over the kitchen noise and I stayed on full alert for any mention of Deviation Road coming under direct fire attack; Sean was at Number 59 on his own. The crews coming in for food, who were watching like hawks for any winds whipping up, kept us well up to date. They told us that water-bombing aircraft were on their way and would focus on preserving the huge power pylons that march through Kinglake, down the mountain, through Strathewen and on to Melbourne. Meanwhile, we kept frying, grilling, chopping and peeling, and found ways around the roadblocks to get food supplies in. The bush telegraph worked wonders: bakery owners from as far away as Healesville brought in van-loads of bread rolls, and the local super-market owner carted anything he could lay his hands on across the road. A truck-load of eskys enabled us to get lunch packs out to the fireline. Without them, many a firefighter was facing up to fourteen hours without food.

My neighbour Julie joined the lunch-making team. We were nervous that we'd left Sean and John at home, but it was understood if Deviation Road was mentioned the aprons were off. My daughter Tania was on the phone constantly from her home in Eltham, about 25 kilometres south-west of us, ordering me to 'Get the hell out of there now!' But there was no sense of panic, just heightened alert. The pub kitchen was filling with smoke and we cooked wearing filter masks, cracking jokes.

Then, without warning, the wind changed and a fireball ripped across the roof of the pub, with deafening noise. We hunkered down inside, contemplating heading for the beer cellar if it got worse. Outside, a bunch of firefighters jumped back on their trucks and threw everything at it. Then they re-formed the food queue and we dished up. All of a sudden, we heard on the ABC that the fire had spotted into Deviation Road. I called Sean on the mobile, raced to the car and made straight for Number 59. Our road was like a war zone: water-bombing helicopters were spraying the Chandlers' bush; strike teams were racing down the easement; there were wall-to-wall CFA trucks. We opened our bores and dams if they wanted to fill up—we knew we'd be taking care of our individual properties. The Smiths rang from Perth, frantic at the news reports they were hearing. We jumped the fence and suggested to Grandpa Bob that he had time to load the kids and dogs and get across to Healesville. We'd do what we could on their property, we assured the Smiths, until they could get a flight back.

A few weeks before the fires, Sean and I had bought the next-door property, Number 1, from Barry Southern. It was a financial stretch, but once we got it to tenantable condition, we figured, it would provide us with good options: we could rent it out to help fund our retirement, or hive it off and sell it. Our insurance broker remarked ominously at the time, 'You'd better insure it before the fire alerts go up, or you'll have a job getting cover', and we did so. But now we made a clear decision: we would defend our house first, but in the event of a major burn we couldn't take care of Number 1 (which was unoccupied) as well.

Sean went into full swing at Number 59: wetting down all the combustible items again, putting out embers as they fell, patrolling constantly, walking across the road to check the fire front, teaming up with John and Julie and Kevin and Rose. Our abiding recollection of that fire is of interminable waiting. Adrenaline levels were up, sleep was out of the question and we steeled ourselves psychologically for any major physical effort that might come. Water containers were full, wet towels were in place. We took naps in shifts, with our boots on, organised shared meals and kept the good humour going.

In the end our properties were untouched, though it was four days before the fire was declared under control. Life quickly returned to normal, but being an analytical lot we frequently revisited our fire plans—that fire was picked over down to the last detail. Our neighbourhood set up its own community fire-guard group, for which the CFA provided a direct liaison officer. We took it in turns to host the training meetings, teasing our CFA contact whenever she tried to raise the subject of how traumatised we might be after the fire. Traumatised? Only when the beer got warm! Or when Rose Chandler couldn't find the tiger snakes that had crawled out of the bush and into her house for safety. We did, though, crank up our regular clearing of anything that would easily ignite and were vigilant about our efforts to burn off and reduce fuel loads.

For the rest of that summer we remained fire-free. Sean and I got stuck into renovating Number 1: more painting, renovating, cleaning and gardening. 'We must be mad,' he declared. 'Here we are again, hacking out blackberries and taking down tree branches, not to mention replacing gutters and tanks.' We confined potential tenants to about half a hectare—enough to mow and take care of—and told the managing agent that they must be made aware they were in a fire-prone area, that they should not consider staying to defend the property, and that they should have contents insurance.

2

An ill wind

DURING 2007 and 2008, the fire-guard meetings continued
and many a barbecue and dinner were defined by conversations about the 2006 fire and the changing weather patterns on
the mountain. It was not just those of us who planned to stay in the
event of a fire who attended the meetings, but also those intending
to go. Other friends, who lived on the Whittlesea–Kinglake Road,
organised their own local fire-guard group. It all seemed to be
working in the spirit of good, responsible community behaviour;
we felt under control.

In late winter 2008 there was a particularly severe snowfall
that stayed on the ground for days, closing schools and roads. This
wasn't normal: it snows most years on the mountain, but rarely
enough to stick. Sitting on the big trees and carpeting the lawns
it did, though, provide some of the most beautiful photos Sean

has ever taken of Number 59. We had them blown up and framed for the hallway.

It was hot early that summer. Sean's precious vegie garden needed daily watering, gum leaves and twigs constantly carpeted the backyard and crunched underfoot like potato crisps, and long strips of bark dangled from the mountain ash as they shucked off any unnecessary baggage. The paddocks were browner than we'd ever seen them and Sean had already decided to slash all the dry grass early. 'We might even get those bloody figs to ripen,' he said of the tree which each year tantalised us with a bumper crop that never quite received enough heat to turn the fruit from green to purple.

The family traffic came and went as usual. My granddaughter Carissa, Tania's daughter, was a regular inhabitant, often with an assortment of school friends; Number 59 had become her retreat from the outside world. Sean would pick her up in Eltham on weekdays and take her to school the next morning. It became the norm to have two or three chattering girls sitting outside under the stars, discussing the meaning of teenage life and later all jumping into a big bed together.

Early 2009 continued the promise of a hot summer. Water levels in the catchments were perilously low; the drought was an unrelenting presence; the air-conditioning seemed to be on constantly. We kept up our usual preparations for the fire season. In one conversation with John and Julie we pontificated that any fires were likely to hit us from the north, given the days of greatest fire danger were those with top temperatures, no rain and the vicious northerlies that put us all on edge. Southerly winds usually spell cooler, sea-breeze-driven changes for us and we look forward to them. 'If anything ever came up from the south through the national park we'd be in strife. Nothing has been burnt in there for years and it's all uphill,' I recall saying. Fire gathers momentum as it moves uphill: give it a tail wind and the speed becomes alarming.

By the beginning of February, the temperatures were hitting the mid-30s. Some days it was hotter in Kinglake than was forecast for the city. But life went on pretty much as usual, with family and friends coming and going; Carissa had reached the stage where half her wardrobe was in her room at Number 59. My nephew Brad had rung in late January to say he was bringing his new partner Sarah over for the Australia v. New Zealand cricket in February and they'd love to visit us the weekend after. They might have another friend with them, he told me. 'Fine,' I said. Savagely hot weather was predicted for the cricket, with talk of a run of days in the 40s. Total fire bans were a given: it was being said that this would be the worst fire season ever. But we'd heard that year after year, ramped up a bit as the drought continued to suck the life out of plant matter across the state. We kept our grass low, slashed paddocks, constantly raked up leaves and bark, and thanked God for the bore water that was keeping the vegies going. We'd never run the air-conditioner so often overnight.

The three days of 40°C hit like an inferno, dry and searing. The drive home through the national park had an ominous feel to it. Trees were dropping branches; you could smell the eucalyptus oil evaporating out of the gum leaves. The grass was brown, the north wind relentless. The car tyres slid on bitumen that had turned to liquid—shimmering in the sun and dangerous to hit. No respite except to stay indoors, with the air-conditioning sapping the power grid. Birds perched on the birdbaths, their beaks open, gasping for air. The horses stayed in their shelter, out of the sun. The dogs weren't moving far. Dust and dirt were blowing in, coating everything.

We prayed for the southerly change. When it finally arrived, around 4 February, we headed outdoors. The 30s temperatures that followed felt like heaven by comparison. But there had been almost a fortnight of temperatures over that—this summer seemed interminable. On Friday 6 February, we started preparing for Brad and Sarah's arrival the next day. There had been days of warnings by the state premier and the emergency services that Saturday was going to be a dangerous day. The messages were clear: temperatures would soar back into the 40s, winds would be gale-force, the fire danger extreme. Victorians were advised to keep off the roads and only venture out if absolutely necessary. If residents in fire-prone areas were intending to leave their properties, they should go early. No specific locations were mentioned at that stage—it was a blanket warning. I'd spoken to Julie about it during the week. 'If anything happens, we'll be ready,' she said.

Sean brought Carissa and a friend up the mountain after school. They were in a bit of trouble over some misdemeanour and were effectively grounded, so it was perhaps more appealing to sit under the stars at Number 59 than be at home deprived of their social life. They had arrived a little grumpy—they'd far rather have been out with their friends—and weren't happy about there being another 40°C day on the way. We ate dinner outside. The stars had never seemed brighter—clear as a bell, a gorgeous sight. The girls were on a quest to spot as many shooting stars as possible, given that each one meant they'd have a wish granted. I kept whingeing about the quantity of dry leaves and twigs—fire fuel—still filling up the backyard, but decided to leave it until the morning, so things would be pristine when our guests arrived. 'I've never seen so much stuff dropping so constantly,' I said to Sean.

An opportunity arose for the girls to spend the Saturday on a property at the bottom of the mountain, where they could swim in the dam and perhaps deal better with the heat. 'I think it's going to be worse outdoors,' I said. 'Besides, you'll have to ask your mother,' I added, flicking a potential flouting of the Friday night grounding back to my daughter. A phone call to Tania brought an emphatic 'No'. Carissa accepted that and we all had a fun night—a lot of banter, teasing and laughs. Life was good aboard the Battlestar and we all slept in peace.

3

Black
Saturday

I T is morning and Sean starts to wet the place down. He gave it a soaking last night too: the watering process has become a nightly after-work ritual. Again he drenches the garden beds, floods the vegies, flicks debris out of gutters. He saturates the areas around the entire house. Carissa starts taking photos of him—she loves our digital camera. The radio is on, tuned to the ABC.

Brad calls and I suggest they might like to change their plans. An air-conditioned hotel room and some indoor shopping might be preferable to a day of intense heat on the mountain. 'We'll be fine, Aunty. Really looking forward to seeing you. In any case, it's pretty damned hot everywhere,' he says. He seems more concerned that the Kiwis lost the cricket yesterday, and that we meet Sarah.

'Is it still okay if we bring my mate Mike with us?'

'No problem,' I say, 'plenty of room for everybody. We're supposed to stay off the roads, so I reckon the earlier Sean comes to pick you up the better. At least we can sit around up here in air-conditioned comfort.' Brad isn't too concerned, and besides, we can wait it out until the change predicted for later in the day. But even now, mid-morning, the air-conditioning is struggling. The thermometer is rising even as we look at it, the wind is gathering speed, there's a heat haze. It isn't going to be pleasant.

Sean heads off to pick up Brad and the others in Melbourne, and is going to drop Carissa's friend home on the way. Tania is planning to join us when she finishes work. She calls from her office in Thomastown, a suburb some 15 kilometres north of Melbourne and about 35 kilometres south of us. 'Nobody's coming in today,' she says. 'The roads were deserted this morning. They've all stayed home and who can blame them. I reckon we'll be closing the doors early and getting out of here.' The heat is already unbearable and the north wind is howling. So much for my efforts to make the backyard look good—it's full of leaves and debris again.

We plan to eat outside later in the day, maybe crash under the cool sycamore. I sweep up another mountain of leaves and put them in the brick firepit for burning later, but they're already blowing out. The gum trees are raining shards of bark. It's so hot—strangling, chest-tightening hot—and it doesn't feel quite right; it just isn't normal. I feel on edge. The air-conditioning is really labouring now, but the only place to be is inside. I do a bit

34

more housework and take a cool shower. Housework: who am I trying to impress? But the beds are ready.

Carissa is chattering, bemoaning the heat. Sean calls to say they've stopped to buy beer and will be back soon, around lunchtime. He says there's plenty of smoke to the north-west of us, towards the township of Wandong on the Hume Freeway, he thinks, but that's a good 40–50 kilometres away. The Hume is the state's main north–south artery and if it has to be closed there will be traffic chaos as motorists seek alternate routes. I hear radio reports of a fire at Kilmore East and Wandong: Julie, who has been in constant touch, is plugged into the fire-alert websites and has the maps out, plotting the fire.

The family spills out of the car around 1.30 p.m. It's great to see Brad again and to meet Sarah and Mike. They're shell-shocked by the heat. 'Man, and I thought it was hot at the cricket yesterday,' says Brad, and he pulls out a large green-and-gold sombrero bought specially for the occasion. I tease him about the fact that he spent a year in the Antarctic and would play golf there in the nude but can't hack a bit of good old Aussie warmth. They pass on lunch—too hot to eat at this point—and Brad and Mike go for a walk in the back garden with a stubby in hand. The dogs take a raincheck on going with them. Unusual: they're always up for an excursion. Sarah stays inside and we have a get-to-know-you chat. She's sensible and nice. Just what Brad needs, I think.

'We can see a fair bit of smoke coming back from the city. They were talking about closing the Hume Freeway,' Sean says.

We discuss where a fire in the Kilmore/Wandong area is likely to head: if there were a northerly behind it, we would see smoke over John and Julie's way, but the sky is brilliantly clear. The radio keeps putting out updates and we don't feel any sense of alarm, because the fire's still far away and heading in another direction, away from us. Other blazes are breaking out across the state, though. 'That's going to stretch things a bit,' I say. Whenever there are multiple fires burning, both ground and aerial firefighting resources have to be carefully deployed to cover as much territory as possible.

Nobody is up for too much activity. The heat is energy-sapping. I flop in a chair on the bricks outside. Brad heads back from the vegie garden and hands me his beer. 'Check out how hot the bottle is. That's amazing: it's undrinkable in a few minutes,' he says. It makes me feel even more uneasy. The wind is like a blast furnace now. Magpies are landing on the lawn with their wings outspread, unable to stay in the air.

'Oh well, we've had a run of days over 40 and this is supposed to be the last one,' I say in hope. I go for a stroll in the back garden to check where the horses are. Some corrugated iron has torn loose from their shelter and is banging in the wind, so I head back in and tell Sean that in this gale it's likely to take off and cut somebody in half. He takes Brad and Mike, and the cordless drill, and they bolt the shelter back together, struggling against the wind. That done, we all gather in the backyard, lethargic. Julie and I stay in touch by phone, continuing to monitor the ABC and the internet. There is now reference to a growing 'Murrindindi complex' fire

(Murrindindi is the name of our shire), but it is still said to be well away from us and burning in the opposite direction. At this stage of the day, we decide to stick at our own properties and forgo the usual drinks-and-dinner get-together later in the day. 'John's bringing the generator down and clearing some things,' Julie tells me. 'We're putting everything in place, just in case.'

The radio says the Hume Freeway has now been closed, as the intense northerly is pushing the fire in its direction. We feel confident that all the reported fire activity is still moving away from us, but we're also very conscious that fires can break out anywhere on a day like this. At around 2.30 p.m. I start to see a plume of smoke, off to the right across the Whittlesea–Kinglake Road. Pure white and voluminous against the vivid blue sky, it seems a long way away. We all watch it for a while, but there's no mention of anything more specific than the 'Murrindindi complex' fire.

Tania calls at around three o'clock to say she's leaving work: they've closed the doors, as it's obvious nobody is venturing out in the heat. She's heading onto Plenty Road, which runs north from the city to Whittlesea, roughly parallel to the Hume Freeway, and plans to come up the mountain that way. I warn her that there might be a lot of truck traffic and that the Hume is closed. We all decide to sit it out until she arrives: we catch up on family gossip, banter about the cricket. Carissa is with Sean, snapping away with the camera.

Half an hour later Tania calls again, sounding distressed. Police have stopped her at a roadblock on the outskirts of Whittlesea.

'Even when I said my daughter and family are up there, they wouldn't let me through. What's the best way for me to get there now?' She's argued with them to no avail. 'They say it's because of the fire further up the Hume Freeway.'

'It will be because they're worried that some idiots will try and get through to the Hume the back way,' I suggest. There are several ways to cut through from Plenty Road to the highway. Tania says she can see a lot of smoke, and given the plume we are seeing beyond the main road we figure it must a fairly significant burn.

I propose to Tania that she turn around and head home if she's feeling uncomfortable. Sean suggests instead that she go back along Plenty Road and take the turnoff east to Arthurs Creek, then come up the mountain through Strathewen. Bowden Spur Road, which leads from there to Kinglake, turns to precipitous gravel but we are all used to driving it. We often refer to it as 'the powerline road' because of the massive pylons that traverse the bush here. It cuts kilometres off the trip to or from Plenty Road, and we use it often for that as well as for trips to the lovely old community hall at Strathewen. Tania isn't confident about making the journey on her own this time, though, given the severe wind and flying branches, and she isn't sure which road fork to take for Strathewen. Sean tells her to go towards Arthurs Creek and he will go down in the Land Rover and meet her there, so she can follow him back up.

Carissa goes with him, the camera still strung around her neck. The colour of the smoke plume has changed: it now has a dirty, yellowish tinge. I ring Julie, who says she's had a visit from a friend who lives near the township and is a veteran firefighter. He's seen the smoke and also doesn't like the colour in it, and suggests we put our fire plans into action now. If the wind changes direction, he fears the fire will head towards us.

The power goes off at about 3.30 p.m. This is nothing unusual for Kinglake, as falling trees and high winds often unplug us. Julie has her battery radio going: 'They mentioned Nutfield might come under attack,' she says, and plots it on her map. Nutfield, near Arthurs Creek, is not a household name, being more a small collection of properties than a township. We agree to make our own decisions to activate fire plans, and swing into action. I suggest that with the extra hands we have at Number 59 we should be able to cope with any ember attacks. If they hit John and Julie first, we can send resources there. Our tight little team has closed ranks.

Sean and Carissa arrive back. Carissa shows me the photos she's taken: 'There's smoke everywhere, and cars. It's horrible,' she says.

'We ran into a huge wall of smoke at the first bend on the powerline road,' Sean says. He tells us how cars were pouring up the hill from Strathewen, and others trying to get down. 'The southern side of the mountain is in flames. We turned around and headed out of there and I kept telling other people to turn back, that they weren't going to get down.' They rang Tania and told her to head back to Eltham, and then raced back here. Sean turns to Brad and Mike. 'We're in seven sorts of shit, boys. Get ready.' He's on the move, wetting things down outside again. Carissa sticks with him, taking photos one after the other. I get Sarah going with a list of fire-plan chores.

My mobile phone rings. It's Tania, she's been waved off the road in Arthurs Creek and is sheltering with a couple in a farmhouse. I freeze momentarily as she describes how a wall of flame is scorching up the mountain. She's telling the man in the farmhouse that her family are up there in Deviation Road. 'He says we're looking towards Deviation Road and that's where it's heading. There are fire trucks tearing along the road down here and the smoke is really thick. I'll stay here. The guy is in the CFA and he seems to know what's going on,' she says. I hear the terror in her voice. 'Okay,' I reply. 'You stay put with them and don't go on the road for any reason. We're cranking up the action. There's no getting out of here now.' And so I have to leave my daughter with strangers, watching a holocaust barrelling towards her family, while I go about getting organised.

I relay to Brad, Mike and Sarah what appears to be happening, which we're still thinking might be an ordinary fire front. 'If it behaves like a normal front, it will roar through quickly and keep moving on. We'll hunker down in the house, or if necessary go across to John and Julie's because that's probably the safest place to be if we can't control it here. Once the front has passed through, then the really hard work begins. We'll be on patrol and putting out spot fires for quite a while,' I tell them. Brad and Mike say they're up for it and look for practical things to do: they're reassuringly strong and capable, and have trained as volunteer firefighters in New Zealand.

Sarah seems nervous and frightened, but keeps her head and calmly asks for instructions. 'I'll do whatever you tell me,' she says. I silently thank God for this sensible, non-panicking person. I tell her to fill the bath, though the water pressure will be low because the power is off and the pumps aren't working, and to take all the large towels out of the linen cupboard and throw them in to soak. I've laid out sets of clothes on the back of the couch in the family room and tell her to put on long pants, a shirt and any boots that fit; the others need to do the same. I ask her to then fill bottles with drinking water, and start packing the wet towels along the bottoms of the doorways in the sitting-room and hallway. She follows all this to the letter, except for the clothes, but I figure she'll get around to that.

Sean has already put on a padded cotton shirt, long pants, and Blundstone boots. I pull on work boots, jeans and the thick Tibetan wool jacket that is my winter security blanket. It's 46°C and I'm dressed for the Himalayas. For some reason, it occurs to me that I haven't put any knickers on. Too bad.

I fill the laundry tub and all our buckets with water and then go outside to pull things away from the house: the outdoor furniture, doormats, a broom, the barbecue. Then I start packing the wet towels along more doorways, slopping water everywhere. We're calm and I'm cracking jokes. Sarah is a bit startled by my fire-alert humour, but it's important to have a laugh if you can. The worst thing you can do in the face of a fire front is panic—it undermines the control and mental strength you are going to need, which can't be overestimated. Fear can paralyse you.

41

I look out the back window. The smoke has turned into a mushroom cloud and has an abnormal motion about it. I ring Julie and tell her we're battening down the hatches, we're on full alert and will fall back to them if we have to. We will pick the safest option to get the others through any approaching fire front, and once the worst of it has gone through and we can get outside again we can rationally attack the spot-fires and ember strikes. I feel quite clinical and logically think things through. I feel guilty about imposing extra stress on John and Julie, but we all decided long ago that their property was the most defendable. 'That place wouldn't move in a hurricane, earthquake or tsunami,' Sean has often said.

With plans in place, we feel quite in control. We are starting to guess at things now. It seems likely that the fire will be coming from the south, which means Number 59 would be hit first. But the wind appears to still be hurtling in from the north: maybe the change in direction has started somewhere else and hasn't quite reached us yet. I know we are on our own. There won't be any emergency services available for the first onslaught; there have been no sirens, no trucks.

The men have gone outside. The pall of smoke is getting bigger and darker: I can see it through the large windows at the back of the house, still seeming distant but starting to block out the sun. The wind is swirling in crazy patterns, objects are blowing around, branches are bending and swaying. The back door is almost wrenched off its hinges every time someone opens it. Crisp leaves and dry twigs are bucketing down, pelting the roof and windows like a hailstorm, filling up the backyard. The lawns are littered.

Even though the air-conditioning has been off for some time, I'm not feeling the heat—too mentally preoccupied. There's still enough gravity feed from the bore's header tank to keep filling the bath. I leave Sarah with her tasks: she must think I sound like an army sergeant, giving orders, matter-of-fact. I always turn into a practical being in times of crisis, and Sean is the same. We trust each other implicitly in that sort of situation.

I grab the car keys off the bench and go to the car to listen to the radio coverage. There's a desperate need to get some sort of handle on where things are. It is stifling out here, hard to breathe even with the car door open and the air-conditioning cranked up. There's no mention of Kinglake, just more about Kilmore and Wandong and Murrindindi. I find it a bit of a confusing jumble of information. It's just after four o'clock: I constantly watch the smoke plume, but still can't pinpoint its exact location. It's off to the right, down near the powerline road, and I'm assuming it is heading elsewhere since the wind appears to still be coming from the north. The weather vane on the chimney is doing a crazy rotation in the gale-force wind, swinging one way and then the next, freewheeling. The wind, howling relentlessly, hasn't slowed and it's impossible to read its direction clearly. I'm hanging out for the predicted wind change.

The smell of smoke is strong now, with a eucalyptus-oil tang to it. The sun is rapidly disappearing. I'm starting to hear a rumble—my hearing has become acute—but it still seems distant. All my senses are on full alert, and the decision to choose fight over flight comes automatically. I don't decide consciously: there is simply no flight response, no desire to leave now. We go with it from here—no thoughts of getting into cars and trying to drive away. I've had it drilled into me that a car is the worst place to be in a firestorm.

Now there is the beginning of a roar, distant and low, like a growling noise with a building baritone edge to it. I look at the weather vane again and it is spot-on south-west. I feel goosebumps despite the sweat that's running down inside my woollen jacket and soaking my heavy socks. My hair is sticking to my face and neck. I've lost track of where Sean and Carissa are, though I know she'll be staying close to him. But I want her to be at what we believe is the safest location in our road and I'm also fretting about Tania in Arthurs Creek, though at least she's in a house with somebody with fire experience. Brad and Mike have climbed onto the roof of the house and are frantically sweeping leaves and twigs off it, though the leaves are falling faster than they can clear them. I feel stressed about the pair being up there in the heat and squalling wind, and abandon the car radio to yell at them to come back down. But they've already made that decision—they've seen a giant ember fall into the paddock at the back of the house and they're shouting and pointing at it. We rush to extinguish it, but there's more coming. I steel myself for the coming battle: there's no doubt whatsoever that we're in for one.

Suddenly, a deafening roar makes me snap my head up in fright. It's an awful noise, like jet aircraft coming in low at full throttle. In less than a second, a strip of the back, main-road boundary has burst into flame, which now starts to spread sideways at an alarming rate. Where the hell did that come from? This is not just the crackle of a fire as it catches dry grass and twigs: angry red shafts are shooting 20 to 30 metres into the air. Flames are curling and swirling, bending to the ground and then flicking up even higher, curving over and flinging balls of fire ahead and into the distance. They rocket over the property like missiles and are dropping like bombs. God almighty, it's going over the top of us, I think. It's a terrifying dance.

But then it starts to skim across the grass in the paddock. This is not normal—the word 'hellfire' comes to mind. I run like crazy into the house, making a beeline for the bath. I count out the number of wet tea-towels needed for everyone's faces and dunk them in the water. Flames are still running down the paddock, skimming across the surface at incredible speed. I think that at least the fire will move on quickly at this rate; it seems to be going too fast to stick. I make the decision to get the others across the road. Sean brings Carissa inside while he chases the spot-fires, and I turn her towards me and hand her a wet tea-towel to tie across her mouth and nose. She is quiet and attentive. I look her dead in the eye, with my hands on her shoulders: 'Take Jazz and go to John and Julie's now. Take Brad, Sarah and Mike with you. Don't stop and don't look back. Just keep going until you reach them. Don't lose the wet tea-towel off your face.'

Sean is yelling at them, 'Go, go, go!' I ring Julie to say they're on their way. She says she'll be waiting at the door; John is outside with the generator going full bore to power the pump for the hoses. It is getting dark; the roar has subsided to a rumble, but the wind is still screaming. Sean prepares to follow the others across the road, taking Harley with him. 'I'm right behind you,' I call. But for a split second I hesitate in the family room. Where's Meg? God, I've forgotten Meg. She's disappeared. I yell her name: no response. I can't leave her here—she can't run like the others, with her old, arthritic legs. What the hell, I'll find her and carry her if I have to. I know this is not what you are supposed to do: you are supposed to save yourself and leave the dog. But I just can't.

The room is filling with smoke. In spite of the wet towels along the doorways, it's billowing in, thick and cloying. A smoke alarm goes off, a piercing, brain-numbing siren. The smoke is making me cough. Where's that bloody dog? Everything outside is catching fire now: I can see the big gum tree out the back flaring and flaming. Shit, I can't go out the back door now. Pitch-darkness rolls down like a blind, in what seems like seconds. For one horrible moment I fear Meg may have taken off outside—she'd follow Sean any- where. But there's no leaving now; I have to stay with the house. The smoke is already noxious and I'm struggling with it despite the wet cloth pressed to my face. I can see, courtesy of the ghastly flickering glow from flaming trees and bushes, that the garden beds are one giant and deadly blaze. The screaming roar is coming back, combining with the smoke alarm in a maddening clamour. My lungs are feeling scorched now and my only thought is escaping the smoke that's getting denser and more bitter to breathe by the second. Mustn't panic; must keep my breathing shallow.

I yell again for Meg, but the very action chokes me. In a last-ditch effort I check the spare room at the back of the house. She's there! Lying low under the piano, not moving, just making the throaty noise she favours when she wants attention. The intelligent eyes are looking at me, her chin resting on outstretched front paws. I try to get her up but she doesn't want to move. She licks my hand and face, though she's not normally a licker. I coax her, but she won't budge, preferring to stay as flat as she can on the floor. I smile to myself and decide she's the smart one: all those 'Crawl low under smoke' messages come into my head. The clever old dog! She's slowed her breathing right down; the wild-dog instinct has kicked in. I lie down on the floor, my arms around her, and she cuddles in and licks my chin. I love this dog.

It's easier to breathe at floor level. I make her start to crawl with me. 'Let's get up the hallway to the bedroom or the study.' I keep talking to her. The bent, arthritic legs aren't liking the crawling motion and she stops to protest. I coax; she licks my hand. The screaming smoke alarm is seriously rattling her—and me, for that matter. She looks up at it with her ears back; I know how she feels—the noise is driving me crazy.

My eyes sting and stream water, my lungs are seriously hurting. Stay low, crawl under the smoke. Above all, don't panic. I have no concept of time—this could be taking seconds, or minutes.

I'm not sure what stage the fire has reached. Has the front gone through? That terrible roar would suggest it is right on top of us. Is the main ember blast still to come? It's pitch-black now. I know the drill: hunker down and wait until the light comes up again and the fire front has fully passed. Then wait a while longer until it appears safe to get out onto burnt ground. Beyond that I have no strategy; I have to deal with this moment by moment. I feel strangely and utterly calm, quite lightheaded in fact, as if I've taken a tranquilliser. I pass the pantry, hauling my hunkered-down dog by the collar, then stand up, feel for a torch and find one, and grab the car keys off the bench. It's not the keys I want, but the tiny LED torch attached to the ring.

More smoke alarms have gone off. The noise is unbearable: the jet-engine roar; huge bursts of exploding yellow light, like bombs going off; screeching alarms; the thump of heavy debris landing on the roof and glancing off windows; things crashing into the side walls. There is a graunching sound of roofing iron moving, as nails and bolts strain, lift and slap down again. Something skids crazily around the backyard and slams against the brick wall.

I head past the spare bedroom and somehow think to grab a woollen blanket. I leave Meg in the hallway, backtrack to the bath and soak the blanket: it seems vitally important to do this. There is enough flickering light from the fire to provide murky visibility. Meg has followed me back and is making a beeline for the piano, agitated and trying to shut her ears. I coax her back and drag her, along with the wet blanket, back to the kitchen. Every breath is agony; the sopping wool weighs a tonne. I can't help thinking that I'm never going to get the water stains out of the carpet, but I'll worry about that later. I seriously want to break the smoke alarms: the continual, piercing screams are making me feel physically sick. I look around for something that will reach one, but no luck. I pull a bottle of water out of the fridge on the way past—suddenly I'm staggeringly thirsty and I need to keep up the fluids.

We get down on the floor in the hallway. To hell with the carpet: I pour water into my hand and Meg slurps it. She's panting heavily. I manage to haul her along, though she's flopped to a dead weight, and the leaden blanket and water bottle are somehow making the journey as well. The smoke alarm outside the main bedroom is totally out of sync with the others, which makes for an even more maddening cacophony. What can I smash it with? It's sheer torment.

We reach the study, but Meg runs back out the door. I can't follow her: all the effort is playing havoc with my ability to breathe and I will myself not to gulp the air in. We are heading into sheer survival mode: I realise I have to leave poor Meg to her own devices, as trying to keep track of her is mentally and physically paralysing. I've done my best for her to this point. The decision makes me feel incredibly sad: the things that dog has survived and now she's in danger of suffocating to death. Then again, she may be fine. I can't dwell on it.

I fall onto my knees in front of the bay-window seat and rest my chin on it. It seems like a huge achievement to have got here;

I need to put my head down and think. I'm still dead-calm, but my heart rate is up, the pulse points thumping, though not from any conscious sense of fear. I have no sense of the temperature either; I'm numb. My mobile phone rings and I drag it from my pocket. It's Sean. 'Is the house all right?' he asks.

'Yes, I'm in the study but it's really hard to breathe,' I reply.

'Just sit tight,' he says. 'The house is the best place to be.'

I feel lumpy in the throat. And where's Meg? I'm afraid she's going to die. Abruptly, I'm brought back to the present with a crash: the ghastly roar has picked up momentum. The bay window offers a shocking view, which hits my brain in slow motion, almost as if this is happening outside of me, like it's somebody else's nightmare. There is an insane hurricane of fire outside; the big trees all through the front of the property are ablaze. I can actually see huge, swirling tongues of burning wind: the air is literally on fire, ripping through everything in its path, searing, swirling, eddying back on itself. It is flinging branches and debris like missiles and the din is increasing. Clouds of red-hot embers are caught in a whirlpool that's glowing ruby and yellow, intensifying as the wind provides a new gasp of oxygen. I crane my neck and look out the bay window to the right. At least the shed hasn't gone up yet. There's paint and petrol in there and God knows what else. It's too close to the house—if the shed goes, the house will too.

A massive branch of mountain ash has fallen across the driveway. It is burning fiercely, crackling and spitting, emitting huge showers of sparks that are at once sucked up into the vicious wind.

The flames have swallowed up the metal front gates and all the other trees are fully ablaze too. Another eddy of scorching embers rushes in from a different direction, hurls pieces of burning branch at the front windows and then savagely swirls the other way. It's like being abandoned in the middle of hell. Suddenly, the heat under my knees is biting through my jeans—the floor is hot, fire-hot. I pull the wet blanket underneath me and sit on it. I consider going to find Meg again, but decide to leave her be. She might already be dead.

The intense glow is lighting up the cars parked in the driveway. Their duco is scorching and blistering, cooking, the tail-lights melting out of shape. I wonder whether the fuel tanks are going to explode and add to the burning projectiles. I am somehow processing what I am seeing; it's being imprinted on my brain; it is terrifying and fascinating at the same time. I must just wait it out—wait, just wait, for the signals that suggest the inferno is moving on. The heat is extreme now: steam is rising off the wet blanket, fogging up my glasses. Man, that's got to be hot! I move off my knees to sit sideways, as my right leg has gone to sleep; I can't feel it at all. My eyes are dry and feeling raw. I unzip my jacket to let some of the moisture evaporate; all my clothes are wringing wet. The high-pitched wailing of the smoke alarms is making me feel deranged and I keep shaking my head to try to restore rational thought.

I don't know what to think. I decide I'm totally in the lap of whatever gods happen to be abroad. Nothing to be done except wait, breathe slowly, wait. I start to concentrate on the others, thankful that they had time to get across to John and Julie's before the worst of it hit. I try to calculate how long it would have taken them, counting the steps, but then decide just to have faith. They're safe, I know they're safe. Sean rang, so they must be there. Don't look at the burning branch: surely Sean got Harley through the gate before that came down. I put my cheek back on the window seat and close my eyes, just let it all go away for a minute. The blanket is drying out underneath me; it's damp and very warm. I'm sweating rivers and want to rip off my jacket.

Distraction, I need distraction. Maybe I should gather up some things. Taking the portable files is part of our fire plan. Not now, though. I realise I've lost the car keys with the little torch: I put them in my pocket while I was wrestling with Meg—they must be in the hallway. I feel slightly panicked without them, can't think straight. At least the smoke here in the study isn't as intense as it is in the family room. There's a wet towel across the bottom of the front door; perhaps that's making a difference. The smoke alarms are making me want to scream. I yell back at them, 'Shut up! Just shut up!'

An exploding noise and huge cracking, breaking sound brings me bolt upright. The massive mountain ash that stands sentinel at the front gate has exploded, snapped right out of the ground. I watch it fall over like a matchstick, its gigantic roots waving in the air. As it hits the road, there's a convulsive shudder that rocks the house. I can't believe it: what sort of force could do that?

Flames start to run across the top of its trunk. This isn't just a fire, it's some monstrous, out-of-control force. 'Shit, it's gone straight through John's front fence,' I say out loud. My thoughts are all over the place. How long have I been here? It seems like hours. The fire isn't passing. Where's Meg now?

The embers are still whipping like crazy. The burning air, with its load of debris, is coming from both sides, hurling itself into a swirling lump in the middle, screaming back up the driveway and towards the front of the house. I duck down below the window seat and hear the fire hit the glass, hungry for new fuel. Is it just doing this here—creating its own frenzied weather? Things must be burning at John and Julie's too, though it's got to be safer there. I put my hands in my pockets. The mobile phone is there, along with the cigarettes. There is no thought of trying to use the mobile. Call who? Nobody is coming to fight this for us; that's a given. I flick it on anyway: it says there's no network. I'm tempted by a cigarette, but tell myself off. Having a smoke in a smoke storm—now there's a good idea!

Instead I turn back to inventorying every other large tree and which way they might be leaning, which one might fall next and hit the house. Where's the safest place to be if that happens? The roofing iron is making loud noises: there's not much I can do about the trees, but what if the roof blows off? I'm starting to feel an edge of panic, thinking about emergency escape routes. Maybe I should kick out the bay window and get onto the driveway, or try to get through the house and out the back door. Stupid, stupid,

stupid: even if I did make it, the radiant heat would knock me out and there's a high probability of more trees falling. Stay with the house, just stay with the house. They don't spontaneously combust. As soon as the front passes, I can get outside and start putting out spot-fires.

Suddenly I can't stand sitting in the study. I crawl to our bedroom next door, for what I don't know, and the floor is hot under my hands and knees, but it's as though just moving and doing something different is somehow constructive. I automatically reach for my jewellery, which is sitting on the bedhead. That makes me laugh: Oh well, if you're going to go through this hellfire, why not wear a diamond bracelet and a Broome pearl? There is no thought of trying to grab anything else. I am still thinking that we will get out, that Sean will be back when the light comes up and we'll fight the fire once the storm has passed.

But I'm extremely agitated and can't settle. The smoke alarms are still driving me crazy. Torture. Moving around is not sensible: it's too hard to breathe, too hot for comfort. I head back to the study. On the way I touch the front-door handle—it's red-hot. Through the glass panels I can see that the entire side garden is burning fiercely and the row of conifers along the fence are flaming like Christmas candles. My poor old antique rose is copping a blast. The front shed will be next to go: amazing that it hasn't already burst into flames. If it does there'll be no exit from the front door: that would be like walking straight into a blast furnace—I'm going to have to get out through the back. Surely there's nothing left to burn on that ground now.

Can't think straight. I have another fleeting thought about grabbing the portable files in the study, and the photos too: I can wheel them out in the plastic bin. But I shelve that idea; we can do it later if necessary. I'm back in the study, kneeling, rocking from side to side and waiting, waiting, waiting for things to change and improve. The wind, the noise, the continuing blast-furnace heat—surely it has to run out of steam soon. Such a prolonged burn is not normal.

A sudden paralysing realisation hits my brain. The horses! Eliza and Ricky are out there with the three goats and they must be screaming. The horror of this is too much to deal with and I try to shove the thought aside. If you can't do anything about it, don't waste mental energy on it now. The idea won't go away, though. They've got room to run and there's the shelter for them to get into—if it's still standing, that is—but the smoke, the noise, the flames will make them panic. Why didn't I think about the horses? It all hit too fast, I suppose. Yet what would we have done with them anyway, except heed the advice we've been given: open all the gates and let them find their own way; don't confine them to a small area. Well, the gates are open, thank God. I hope against hope that they don't run into barbed wire or try to jump anything in the dark. As soon as I can get out, I'll check on them. But I feel sick at the thought and it spins my head out; I want to vomit.

Suddenly there's a chink of light, it seems blinding and all my attention turns to it. Woo-hoo! I've been waiting for this. It is coming from ground level and slowly, slowly, begins to push the darkness upwards. It's surreal, as if a powerful spotlight is being shone along the ground, creating a clear line below the darkness. I feel excited beyond belief—this is it! It's starting to calm down. I just have to wait until it creeps further up.

But then, almost as abruptly, the line of light shuts down again, as if somebody has flicked a switch. Another huge blast of scorching embers whirls in from the left: this damned thing is coming from a different direction now, as strong as ever. Everything is still swirling every which way, branches are beating on the roof, iron is flapping. God, don't tell me there's another front coming through. The smoke alarms scream on and on and on. Why haven't they chewed up the batteries with all that blaring? I'm almost getting used to the competing noises, but the light shutting down is almost unbearable. More waiting. The new front is attacking the front shed and the western side of the house, ripping through the dark.

I don't know how long I've been watching for. Then, all of a sudden, that line of light is coming back. There it is again at ground level, lifting the gloom. I zero in on the cars in the drive. They're looking like a Dali painting: elongated, abstract versions of their real selves, the door handles melted down the panels like candle wax. The airbags have gone off in Sean's car. I hear crackling noises now: to the right, the front shed is burning, flames darting out under the corrugated iron. The wind is still howling at full strength. But above the din I seem to hear my name, ever so faintly. I decide it's some sort of trick: my ears have been seriously assaulted and maybe I'm hearing things. I tune out, but it gets louder. Somebody really is screaming my name: 'Jane! Jane! Where are you?' It's unreal; I must be imagining it. Nobody could have got through that fiery nightmare out the front, where everything is still flaming viciously, the big toppled tree now one giant bonfire. I find myself wondering, for a split second, how long the road is going to be blocked by that one. Then the voice penetrates again: 'Jane! Jane!' I shake my head. It's Sean, and he's yelling from somewhere at the back of the house. I feel joyous—if he's made it back here, it must be safe outside. From what I can see, the fire doesn't seem to have died down any, but he's here—he's here! I don't have to do this on my own any more.

I run like crazy down the hallway, leaving the blanket behind, yelling back that I'm on my way. To my astonished relief, Meg pops up beside me! She's heard him too and is eager to follow. As I enter the kitchen, the smoke hits me like a brick: it's extremely thick and has a sharp, unbreathable, toxic edge to it. Poisonous. The kitchen window is framing Armageddon.

There's still some light, though. On the way through I notice my handbag on the kitchen bench and sling it over my shoulder. Can't find the car keys; they're still up the front somewhere. It's an automatic reaction: the bag and the keys. I put the keys out of my mind.

The journey seems interminable. I reach the bathroom and detour in to grab a wet towel, since we are going to need it. The water in the bath is hot. Sean yells that he's fighting the fire outside the laundry. 'Are you okay enough to get out here and help me?' But the poisonous smoke is taking the lining off my throat and hitting my lungs like burning acid; it's painful and frightening. I am fighting to keep going—another lungful and I'll shut down. 'I can't breathe!' I yell back. There's a fine line between coping and wanting to just keel over and choke. I breathe into the wet towel, which provides some relief though the fabric is hot; it's like breathing through soup. My eyes are streaming again.

'Can you make it to the back door?' Sean calls out. 'Everything's on fire out here.'

I make it to the entrance of the laundry, to be greeted by a bizarre noise. A loud hissing, with a hollow roar behind it, like air coming out of one of those high-pressure hoses. I look in, but reel back: where the washing-machine hose outlet goes into the laundry tub, a vicious flame is rushing out, as if from a blowtorch. The hose has melted away and the tongue of bright orange fire is scorching up the wall behind the tub, turning it black.

'It's burning in here,' I shout to Sean. With all my force, I instinctively throw the heavy, wet towel at the fire, in a full-on, overarm, well-aimed pitch. Splat! The weight of it wrenches my shoulder. There's a loud hiss and steam rises. Every breath is agony now. I'm sucking in vaporised plastic and the petrochemical smell is palpable. I can see Sean outside, silhouetted against the laundry window, beating at the flames like a madman. I grab the towel again and smack it against the scorching wall, which sizzles and steams. Sean yells over the racket to say he's got the fire under control outside. I scream back that I've put the flames out in the laundry tub and I'm coming out. I can't breathe, can't see and can't stand this much longer. I'm one gasp away from blacking out. But I feel like we've struck a major blow; we're working in unison and ready for the next round.

Taking the wet towel with me, I race straight for the back French door and Meg slides out beside me. No time for emotional reunions: Sean is beating out flames at the side of the house, shovelling dirt at them like a machine. He says that if he can get down the side and attack the timber verandah, he can keep the flames from the house—chop off the wooden verandah somehow. He whirls around, but then stops dead: 'The axe and the chainsaw have gone up with the back sheds,' he says. It strikes me as a crazy plan, too big and risky a task in these conditions, but he won't stop.

'Just leave it,' I scream at him over the wind and the roar. The radiant heat is horrendous: any exposed skin feels ready to be peeled off. Sean will fry if he goes any closer to the front shed. The Land Rover is in the carport next to it and if that explodes while he's down there he'll be trapped. He won't give up, though, and keeps shovelling dirt, flinging it as hard and as far as he can, stamping on other smaller fires to put them out. The conifers along the side fence are still burning strongly. I notice with horror that the large water tank near the front shed has disappeared. It has completely melted; there's nothing left. 'Where has all the water gone?' I ask Sean. 'Evaporated before it hit the driveway,' he yells. I'd left a large tub of water outside during our early preparations and it too has vaporised. The full tank next to the kitchen is on fire, with the water still in it.

Again I scream at Sean to leave it, just leave it, there's nothing we can do with a shovel and a wet towel. But he continues to fight the monster, insisting that he can still beat it. I want to fall in a heap, but I continue to pull him back. The Land Rover is burning now, flames from it licking out from the carport. 'My drum kit's in the back,' Sean says. It's his pride and joy. He hesitates in the face of the vicious onslaught and I head for the vegetable garden at the back and to the left of the house. I sit on the brick steps that lead up into the vegie garden and can see the flames slipping under the front steps and verandah, licking under the timber. I'm going to sit here and watch our house burn down. The fire is howling, buffeting, smoking, and things are still catching alight. Except, that is, for the vegetable garden: it's a small haven, flattened but not yet destroyed. The lemons are cooking on the tree, roasted and browning nicely. I mourn the tomatoes.

I sit on the top step, feeling defeated, and watch Sean doggedly fighting the flames. Meg has parked herself on the grass. Sean walks towards me, looking angry. He rages at the fire, furious that this thing is beating him. He heads back towards the side garden and keeps on with the shovelling and cursing. 'I'm not giving up. We can get this under control,' he yells through the wind. While

I'm watching him, a strange thing happens: I suddenly feel an overwhelming compulsion to call somebody neutral in the outside world. Not a relative—my first thought is work. I'm not going to make it there on Monday, and I need to let them know. It's partly that entrenched work ethic, which discourages you from letting people down. It's more than that, though: I need someone outside to be aware that we are here, trapped. We still may not make it out of this—it's far from over. Trees are starting to explode along the side fence.

I automatically dial my publishing director, James. We always enjoy a joke and a laugh; we're good at bouncing off each other and, besides, I know he will be businesslike about informing people and keeping tabs on our situation. He answers and I ask him to guess what I'm doing; he thinks I've been enjoying a few Saturday afternoon drinks. I tell him that I'm sitting watching my house go up in flames. 'You are kidding, aren't you?' he says. I tell him that I doubt if I'll be at work next week because we won't have a house, that I don't know how long we're going to be trapped here, that I'll get back in touch when I can. I just want him to handle that side of things, keep things ticking on the work front and let my workmates know what's going on. Apart from that, I have no recollection of the conversation. But I feel an overwhelming sense of relief that I've made connection off the mountain—one less thing to stress about. When I hang up, I wonder why the mobile network is back on. But I feel reassured and able to face whatever is ahead.

Sean joins me at the steps and suggests we get across to John and Julie's. 'The fire is in the wall cavity, which means it's invaded the structure now. I can't get down the side,' he says. Neither of us is keen to turn our burning house into a spectator sport; the feeling of being beaten is debilitating. The surrounding environment is too dangerous and unstable: trees are still falling, windows will shatter soon, the heat and smoke are deadly. There's no safety here, with parts of the garden flaring into flame again as each breath of wind brings intense, renewed activity. We feel overwhelmed.

Sean detours back through the vegie garden. It's hard to make out whether the horses are there: the smoke is too thick. We reunite at the steps, Meg sitting beside me patiently. We head across to the scorched side lawn. 'Stay on the ground that's already been torched,' Sean says. On the way, he tells me the others all made it across the road. When Brad, Sarah and Mike reached the pine trees on John's front verge, though, they started to panic, he tells me. Carissa was screaming at them to follow her, but they stopped. 'I had to get through the front garden because the trees had come down on the driveway,' Sean continues. 'I only just missed the big bugger falling across the road. Talk about split-second timing.' Hearing the others yelling in terror, he had gathered them up as he went past. After the main fire front and ember strike went through, they all began attacking the spot-fires.

Refocusing on the present, he says, 'I'll come back for the horses and goats. Let's just get the hell out of here before it's too late.' We continue down the side lawn—it seems like a very long walk.

Meg stays with us, bent old legs pumping: no way is she going to be left behind. We reach the post-and-rail front fence, which is still on fire. Sean kicks out a section with one swift boot, and it crumbles: we are on Deviation Road. Keeping clear of the huge fallen tree, we make it to the other side and onto the grass verge on John's front boundary. We can't get to a gate and John's steel fence is the next obstacle. If we can get over that, we'll then have to skirt the pine trees behind their house, which are now ablaze.

Sean reaches through the mesh and starts trying to wrench the fence open with his bare hands—rigid steel mesh, stapled with heavy-duty connectors. But he does it! I'm dumbstruck and wonder where he's dredged up that strength from. I get through the opening; he carries Meg and puts her down on the other side. I look back over my shoulder to see our house fully alight. From this perspective, it's starting to throw out an intense glow. 'It's gone. Just don't look. It's gone,' he says dejectedly. I feel like our world has gone mad.

We walk down the blackened grass of John's paddock and head towards the house. I spot John near the concrete water tank at one end of the house, madly hosing and whistling as hard as he can. 'He's stressing about you still being across the road,' Sean says. Running towards me across the paddock now is Brad. He's dropped what he is doing and is racing flat-out towards me. 'Aunty! Aunty!' he yells over the wind, and crushes me in a bear hug, just about lifting me off the ground. 'I thought you were a goner.' He is shaking from head to foot, in shock. 'Not me, buddy, but the house certainly is,' I tell him. 'I've never been so glad to see somebody in my life,' he declares.

John looks up, waves nonchalantly and keeps on hosing and whistling, the generator at full crank—it is the only thing keeping the water pumps going. The pine trees are glowing and swirling in the wind, Julie's prized garden is smoking and wilting, the stand of bush further down the property is flaring and candling. The thick smoke obscures everything else.

We put Meg into the laundry with Jazz and Harley, and fall through the French doors into the family room. Brad and Mike stay outside with John, tackling the flames. Carissa bolts off the couch when we come in and can't decide who to hug first. 'You've been gone so long,' she says. Her words tumble out: 'I'm so scared. I didn't drop Jazz on the way over. The others wouldn't follow me. I thought I was going to die on the road, so I just had to keep running. I could feel the fire on my back. It was burning my hair.' We just keep hugging and reassure her that we're all going to be fine.

Julie and Sarah are bustling from room to room, checking under doors. On patrol. Now is not the time for a full debrief. 'Hi Jane,' Julie says, before beetling back up the hallway. I let rip a nervous laugh—it's as if I've just ducked over for a coffee, she's so calm and collected. But I need to take a breather, unscramble my thoughts, find out where Tania is. Carissa tells me she's still in Arthurs Creek. Thank God for that. 'I was on the phone to Mum while the fire was outside,' Carissa says. 'Everything was glowing really red. I told her you were still across the road and that Sean had gone to get you. She just kept yelling at me, "Where are they? Where are they?"' I try Tania's mobile number and can't connect, but I send a text message anyway in the hope it will reach her. I have no idea of the time: the smoke is blocking out what little light there is left. Sean has gone outside again and I assume he's with John, continuing to damp down the burning garden. The pine trees are a huge worry.

Julie and I swing into practical mode. The local maps are still spread out on the dining table. From the information we already have, we try to determine where the fire front might have gone and how much territory is still under siege. Julie puts her hand on my shoulder. 'It's terrible. Your house is gone,' she says.

It's starting to get dark and the searing heat is bit by bit reversing into a weather pattern that at least feels comfortable. 'That southerly change didn't cool down the fire or drop its speed at all,' I say.

'You've always said that if anything came up from the south, through the national park, we'd be in for it,' Julie says. But now she's worried that another front might whip back on us from a different direction. We've given up listening to the battery radio for now. No point: we're still in the middle of a hellfire, with nowhere to go. Quite rationally we discuss the fact that we are going to be here for some time, and we start to sort out food and water supplies. It's a natural instinct for both of us to plot out the catering requirements, keep our group of people calm and, of course, as safe as possible. I'd kill for a cup of tea, but instead we are drinking litres of water. There's no power for cooking, but there's plenty of tinned food and the thawing freezer offers up loaves of bread. 'At least the dogs are going to be well fed,' Julie says. We are prepared for a long, long night.

'There are trees down all along the road,' I tell Julie. 'Sean said on the way over that the Smiths' house has already gone, but he couldn't see as far as Number 1. We're pretty much trapped here.' Power lines are swinging in the wind. Julie and I flop on the lawn in front of the house again and examine the state of affairs. Food is sorted; water is sorted; people can sit down and rest, regroup. The situation of our neighbours is unknown: the Chandlers managed to call Julie to say they're alive but ringed by fire and fighting it. Our mobiles are ranging in and out of network coverage. We check intermittently but desperately try to conserve battery power. What lies ahead can't be fathomed.

It suddenly occurs to me to ask, 'Where's Bertie?' John and Julie's much-loved black cat and our three dogs probably aren't a good combination. Sure enough, Bertie's retreated under a bed. But at least he's been accounted for—he's part of the tribe too.

Julie tells me how Carissa was the first to get here from Number 59, collapsing through the door. Terrified, breathless, still clutching little Jazz, she told John and Julie how she'd got to their gate and kept screaming at the others to follow her. She asked John if we were all going to die, and he told her she wasn't going to die as long as he kept whistling. 'At the gate she looked back over her shoulder,' continues Julie, 'and saw Sarah knocked right off her feet by the blast of the fireball.' Scrambling to get Sarah up, the others had momentarily panicked and dived under the pine trees. Carissa had to make the decision to keep going before she collapsed. It was a split second later that Sean ran into the others on his way across the road and led them to safety through the back door of John and Julie's house. The garden was on fire and Harley disappeared in the smoke, doubling back to the house. 'Brad, Sarah and Mike only made it to the house by seconds,' Julie tells me.

According to Julie, Harley reappeared soon afterwards and ran straight to the whistling, hosing John. Sean had little choice but to get the group indoors and return outside to fight the flames with John while the firestorm played out its vicious dance. They received some protection from the clay bank at the back of the house, and the large concrete tank. Once the worst of the front had passed, Sean began his repeated attempts to get back across the road to find me, John hosing him down from head to foot beforehand.

'I didn't have time to notice what was happening outside,' Julie says. 'All I could do was concentrate on getting everything blocked up inside.'

'Just as well, probably. You really didn't want to see what was going on out there,' I reply.

The enormity of what we are in the middle of is like a dream. We have all gathered outside, not sure where best to escape the smoke and confusion. John and Sean are still on constant alert outside, wetting down everything they can. There is no concept of anything beyond our immediate environment and the rest of the road. Julie is stressing about our other neighbours. Next door, the Cahill family are all there—the parents, two adult sons, and an adult daughter, her partner and one-year-old baby boy. Julie spoke to them earlier, before the flames hit, and suggested mother and baby come across the road just in case anything got out of hand. It's well and truly out of hand now.

Miraculously, Julie's landline is still working. Neighbours are trying the 000 emergency number constantly, but can't connect. Julie's ringing around to see who might need help. We can't leave, as there's no way off the property, but people might be able to join us in this safer haven if they can get through or across the paddocks. The bush surrounding the Chandlers is burning fiercely; they only have one way out and it's blocked by fire. Nobody answers their phone and we figure they'll be outside putting up the good fight—we convince ourselves that's the case. I'm worried about our next-door neighbours, the Smiths, and the tenants at Number 1. The Smiths have always vowed to leave in the event of a fire, because of Dionne's chronic asthma and their concern for their children's safety.

Our tenants, a family with three teenage girls, who moved from the city because they wanted more space for their beloved pets, might have stayed because of the air-conditioning we'd put in the house. I've spoken to them about fire planning, but feel anxious about how they'd have handled this sudden onslaught if they were home. They probably wouldn't have known what to do. I've assumed the Smiths have gone, and our tenants understood that they shouldn't stay under such circumstances, but I should have followed through. I realise that's a big flaw in our fire plan. It would have made sense to ask our immediate neighbours whether they were planning to stay or go on a 46°C day of howling northerlies. At least that way we'd know who to look for and who was safely away. 'I'll write that into my revised plan,' Julie says, and I determine to do the same.

Right now, though, the reality is that we are sitting on a semicircle of lawn completely surrounded by fire. A ringside seat in the middle of an inferno, watching the distant glow of our burning house and hoping to God that four other families are okay. That hope is severely dented as we suddenly glimpse, through the smoke and dusk, headlights coming down the Cahills' drive. 'Please tell me they aren't trying to get out,' I say to no one in particular.

'God, they won't see the trees on the road. There's zero visibility out there,' says Sean, in horror. 'The big ash that's down—they'll run straight into it,' he adds.

There's no way the Cahills can see us, no way to warn them. It's like watching a horror movie as we see the car run up a bank at the end of the drive, headlights pointing skywards. But then it reverses back down and heads back to the house. We all slump with relief.

The incident leaves us feeling shattered and stunned. Nobody is saying much. Nobody is really processing much—it's a case of just dealing with one issue at a time. We have no idea how long this fire is going to continue, how widespread it is and what degree of danger we are still facing. We take it moment by moment.

Sean and John continue to run the generators outside; our ability to keep the property safe depends on them. Sean has already been back across the road once to find the horses and goats, and decides to head there again. 'They're alive,' he says. 'I saw them in the paddock near Number 1. I'll try and get them into the vegetable garden area, as it's still okay. They were too spooked to come near it before.' Julie and I start a practical list of things do. Energy, we all need some energy. We rustle up bread and jam, but nobody can eat—except for the three dogs, who are happy to scoff whatever's offered. Harley is coughing badly. It's a dry, hacking cough that is making him retch, and he gulps water constantly; he's caught a lot of smoke. He's also limping a bit. I check his paws, but can't see anything on the black fur and foot pads. He's just up for a big lick, cuddle and tail-wag. All the dogs are drinking water continuously. Julie resorts to handing around a large bowl of almonds. 'They'll give us some energy,' she says.

The New Zealand contingent assess what they have left behind. Sarah had the foresight to grab her backpack containing her and Brad's wallets, passports and airline tickets, but Mike is left without any documentation. They are still in shorts, sandals and T-shirts. Sean reappears from Number 59. The horses and goats are still upright, he tells us, but he thought they'd take fright if he tried to move them and that would be too dangerous, so he left them to it for the time being.

There is nothing we can do except wait, and keep patrolling and fighting whatever's still burning or catching fire. The emergency services are going to have to cut their way in. We know our environment: the mountain must be sealed off from the outside world, with no easy roads in or out. We turn the battery radio back on and hear that there are reports of Kinglake being under fire attack. 'What the hell?' Sean says. 'They've just found out? There was no mention of us before we got hit.' Well, at least they now know we're in big trouble, I think.

The darkness has come down like a blind. The atmosphere around us is eerie, the orange light from Number 59 still illuminating part of the road. 'Those blue flames we can see are probably my DVD collection,' Sean says somewhat cynically. The wind has died down a bit and now we can hear regular faint explosions in the distance. 'Gas bottles going up,' Sean says. The smoky air is still giving our eyes and lungs hell. We drag some spare mattresses onto the lawn so everyone can lie down. We can't tell whether night has fallen or if we are still operating in a dark haze from the fire. The light is unnatural; the world looks unrecognisable.

It's strange, the sudden contrast between the deafening roar of the fire front and the sounds of its aftermath—now there is just a continuing crackle rather than incendiary blasts. All normal human-related activity has disappeared: there are no cars, no lights, only lines of fence-posts glowing in the dark, trees popping and spitting with flames. There is a wider, ominous gleam overhead, which lets us see beyond our property up to the Whittlesea–Kinglake Road. Houses are burning there.

'It just keeps going,' I say to the others. 'Things are still catching fire.' The monster remains hungry.

We put Carissa to bed inside. Numb and traumatised, she just wants it all to go away; hopefully she's exhausted enough to sleep for a while. She lies down, but keeps her clothes and boots on. The rest of us stay on the lawn, taking turns to patrol the most threatening fire spots. The explosions are becoming more audible now, some close, some distant. Gas cylinders, cars, fuel containers—one bang after another, echoing and competing.

We matter-of-factly discuss what might be causing particular sounds. Trees are snapping and falling as the flames undermine them, some hitting the bitumen with a thud and others crashing in the bush. There's a crazy move to count the number of trees falling in John and Julie's stand of bush or landing on our road. There's another sound too, that of buildings imploding—a hollow thump as a roof collapses and takes walls with it, then a muffled crash as the structure hits the ground. We've very quickly learnt to tell the difference between the noises of this night.

Suddenly there is a louder than usual explosion from the direction of the main road. A cloud of thick black smoke, with a menacing bright glimmer to it, spirals up and illuminates everything. 'Bloody hell. That's diesel and tyres,' John says. 'They'll keep burning for ages.' There are constant secondary explosions: drums of fuel being hurled, hissing and blowing out as the heat expands the gases to bursting point. I start to worry about the toxic smells. What are we all breathing in? Arsenic from treated pine, fuel and rubber, polystyrene, melted plastic and God knows what else that we are told lurks in buildings and can kill you. None of it smells or tastes good, that's for sure. Our eyes are dry and painful. Sean is starting to cough and wheeze, and there's nothing here for his asthma.

We go back to the interminable patrolling and waiting. Sean asks Brad to go back with him across the road for another attempt to confine the horses so they don't run through the damaged fences and onto the road. He doesn't feel confident about doing it, so I go with Sean instead. We leave John on fire patrol, still whistling, and head over to Number 59, already adept at skirting burning debris. The hole left by the uprooted mountain ash at the front gate is spewing sparks and smoke like a mini volcano. I don't really look at the smouldering house. The water tank near the kitchen is still burning, outlined against the dark. We pick our way through to the vegetable garden. Sean does that adrenaline thing again, ripping the wire clothesline apart with his hands. He's looking for something to make a temporary enclosure for the green oasis. Sheds and trees are still burning just across the fence on the neighbouring property—we're going to have to patrol here throughout the night to keep the horses safe.

Sean goes into the dark paddock to find them; there's still enough fire glow for reasonable visibility. Suddenly they loom up in front of me as he herds them in—our Clydesdale Eliza and Ricky, the black thoroughbred we adopted after he'd been found abandoned. They're snorting and still agitated. Eliza's white leg 'feathers', a distinctive Clydesdale feature, have been burnt off and she looks a little bald in that department; Ricky's mane and tail are singed and he's coughing. They come for a pat and are happy to be on unburnt grass. They appear to be walking okay.

Eliza doesn't let the opportunity pass her by and heads straight for the cos lettuces in the vegie beds. The fact that they're still there is miraculous. We laugh—she's contentedly having a salad in the middle of a nightmare, her munching audible. She jumps at another explosion, but quickly returns to the succulent greens. Under normal circumstances it would be cause for immense horse-and-goat rage if any of them got loose in the vegie patch, but right now there's little point in getting stressed about it.

The goats choose to stay in the paddock, their white coats a crazy contrast against the black, like they're glowing in the dark. They don't appear to have a mark on them, not even a patch of soot or a singed spot. 'That's bloody amazing. I'm following them next time,' Sean says. I'm avoiding the chook run; there is no way they could have survived that much heat and smoke. But we laugh again as one of the tamest of the little brown girls comes clucking out of the henhouse. There's no fence left around it, but the chooks are all alive and seemingly well. Amazing. They start to scratch in the charred earth.

We feel good. All our creatures are alive. A full check will have to wait until dawn. This fire isn't over yet: burning structures are still visible across the main road, and trees are still catching. We head back to John and Julie's. Harley goes into a crazy greeting when we arrive. His paws are burnt but he's still running like clockwork! He flops down and we try to keep him quiet so I can wrap his paws in wet towels, but he resists treatment and we have to go with that and just try to keep him still. Try doing that with a boisterous black labrador affectionately known as 'the Bulldozer'.

It's now around 11 p.m. I flop on the lawn for a few minutes and we all debrief again. Our mobiles are flashing in and out of 'No network' mode. Tania got through to Carissa earlier, apparently, and told her she's out of Arthurs Creek and back in Eltham; at least she knows we're all alive. While we are still on the lawn, there's a massive explosion. 'That must be the service station,' we say, almost in unison. It means the town is still going up. It seems like a natural conclusion and we're resigned to it.

I go to check on Carissa, but she's already bolted out of a troubled sleep and seen the still-glowing trees through the window, and comes staggering into the family room. She's terrified the trees are going to fall and hit the house. Sean puts her on one of the outdoor mattresses and cuddles her, hiding her head, shutting out the view. She clings onto him and stays still. She just wants to go home. 'We'll get you out of here as soon as it's safe, mate,' Sean tells her.

It suddenly feels very cold. We've plummeted from that hellish 46°C to something bordering on chilly; now I'm grateful for the Tibetan jacket and boots. My years working in news media tell me that we must be a headline by now. People will be worried;

emergency services must be on the way. But I quickly lose any concept of that faraway, outside world; we've got a long survival battle ahead of us still. We're conserving the batteries in the radio and only tuning in for periodic updates, which just repeat that Kinglake has been hit by fire. Hit? We're still in the middle of it.

Brad and Sarah crawl into bed and Mike falls onto a mattress in the lounge; Carissa stays with Sean. We remain on full alert. Suddenly I jump up: 'I've got to walk down the road. Can't stand sitting here wondering what's happened to the Smiths and the tenants. I've got to go.' John says he'll come with me. I try to dissuade him, but soon a seventy-year-old diabetic Greek and a pumped-up middle-aged woman are heading for the front gate. 'I'll just go as far as the corner,' I yell back at Sean. 'If anybody is trapped we might be able to get them back here.' John has strapped a torch on his hat, like the ones you see on coal-miners' helmets. 'Trust you,' I tease, 'a bloody gadget for every occasion.' We laugh, but the device makes sense, leaving his hands free.

The explosions all around us are still constant. At the front gate we turn left, heading for the Smiths. Suddenly we run into toppled power poles, lying sideways at crazy angles, the wires snaking all over the road. 'They'll be okay. The power has been out for hours,' John says. I'm not convinced and gingerly pick my way through, trying to avoid stepping on anything, like a childhood game of hopscotch. The unoccupied property next to John and Julie's is a pile of rubble. On the right is the Smiths' driveway; it's obvious that the house has gone. The property up on the main road provides a backdrop of spewing black and orange fire. 'How much stuff has that bloke got up there? Must be a decent-sized fuel dump,' John says. Dionne's car is sitting at the top of the driveway, a burnt-out frame. 'The other cars aren't there, though,' I say to John.

He goes up the driveway anyway. 'Is anybody here? Is anybody here?' he calls. No answer, just an eerie silence. 'They're not here. Let's go and check Number 1.'

We get back onto Deviation Road. The roadside trees are still burning and we can see the glow from Number 1. John stops and turns to me, his shoulders slumping. It's a look I know well. 'I was really worried about you all the time you were at Number 59. I would have been really pissed off if anything had happened to you,' he says. Enough said. We just smile and walk on. Past the small cottage occupied by an elderly woman: no car there. My legs feel weightless; I'm half-running now, desperate to get to Number 1. Silhouetted in the glow I can see three dead goats—on their backs, legs in the air, burnt black. The house has disappeared. John runs up the long drive calling for any signs of life. Again, silence. 'Their animals have fried. Look for a car up the back,' I urge him. 'Nope, no cars here,' he yells.

My legs won't stop. I'm heading for the township, usually about a forty-minute walk. 'You go home, John. I'm going to see what's downtown and tell them we've got a group of people in Deviation Road.' That exasperated look again: he's not turning back. But I'm worried about the exertion, his high blood pressure. 'Come on, love, let's just keep going,' he says. 'I'll be okay.'

We make the main road and turn left. There's one wall of the Catholic church left standing just around the corner—the back wall with the window in the shape of a cross, now etched against the ongoing glow. The rest is rubble. Past the nursery café on the right, where trees are still burning fiercely, the pretty cottage gone. A scene appears in front of us and we stop dead. A massive mountain ash is lying across the main road. To the right of it there's a car on its side in the deep culvert; smashed head-on into the tree are two other cars, burnt out. Branches are still smouldering. We can clearly see a motorbike under one end of the tree, and evidence of more cars on the other side. It's a moment of terror and panic frozen in time.

I walk over to the car in the culvert. There are no signs of life here at all: we don't need to say a word—the occupants have either got out and run or they've been vaporised. I stare in horror at the burnt-out station wagon—is it our tenants' car?

'Nothing we can do with any of this at this moment,' John says. The only way through is to climb over the tree. I squeeze and manoeuvre my way through the gaps; John clambers over the trunk. We talk about scenes like this that we've experienced in battle zones. I've worked in a few and John, having grown up in the Middle East, has also seen his share of destruction. We instinctively know not to look at any human shapes: it's a sight that never leaves you. 'How long ago do you think this happened?' I ask. 'Nobody seems to have been here yet.' I flip open my mobile. No bloody network, no bloody point. The phone lines and mobile towers must have melted.

The sound of fire crackling is all around us. We push on and reach the first houses on the main road. A two-storey is ablaze, but others in front of it are intact. Cars are burnt out in driveways, gas cylinders are going off, fences are flaming, trees are creaking and groaning. 'It's all so unstable,' I say to John, but I have to keep going. There is absolutely no sign of human life. On the left, another scene stops me dead. 'The SES has burnt. The trucks are still in the shed. They didn't have time to get the bloody trucks out of the shed,' I say to John. 'What the hell are we going to find from here on?' The roof has caved in on the charred emergency vehicles. My legs are moving instinctively—no physical sensation, just pumping on and on. The old sawmill to the left is on fire, a mountain of logs ablaze. The Singhs' vegetable packing sheds have collapsed too. Past Shelley Harris Court on the left, its nestled houses still on fire. I'm hurtling towards the pub now, John keeping pace behind me. The Greek and a crazy woman looking for what, I don't know.

The pub is still standing. The houses opposite it, on the right, are either ruins or just starting to burn. Our friends Milan and Jelena Strmota's house has disappeared, but I can see their shop is still there, as is the supermarket. We race to the pub carpark, which also houses the CFA shed. It is wall-to-wall cars; stunned people are standing around, some listening to battery radios, no one saying a word. They just look at us dumbfounded. We quickly take it in. 'Nothing we can do here, love. Let's head back and sit tight,' John says. The extent of it all is almost beyond us.

We head back up the main road. A pile of firewood on a front verandah has caught fire since we came down. I point it out to John. 'Leaving firewood at the front door,' he rails. 'Bloody morons!' It's a silent walk from there. Going up this hill would normally have me grunting, but instead I'm flying along.

Our world is glowing and exploding, and I'm starting to worry about the big trees falling. We have to get back through the collapsed giant ash. As we approach it, we see headlights through the smoke. There's a car heading down the still-burning culvert, a four-wheel-drive, snaking around debris, picking a path through the smoke. It screeches to a halt when we wave our arms, and the driver's window goes down: it's Lorraine Casey, who lives up on the main road and is one of our chatting-over-the-fence friends.

'It's you, Lorrie. Where on earth have you come from?' I ask.

She looks blank. 'I've got to get Wendy to the CFA, she's going to fucking die on the back seat of my car,' she says in her strong Scottish accent. 'She's burnt and can't breathe. ' I look in the back window and see someone in the distinctive yellow CFA jacket, lying face-down on the seat. 'Are you guys okay? Do I need to get you down there too?' Lorrie asks. 'We're fine. Just go,' I say. Her car sprays dirt as she accelerates around the fallen tree and bounces onto the bitumen at full throttle. Hell is still unfolding.

As we approach the corner of Deviation Road, more head-lights loom through the smoke. There's another huge tree down a little further up the road. We see the flashing red and blue lights of emergency vehicles. 'I can hear a chainsaw,' I say to John. Sure enough, we stand and watch a chunk of the tree being cut away. Men in bright overalls have hammered out a section big enough to get a car through. A police car inches towards us through the opening, then stops and the officer winds down his window. 'There's eight of us trapped in Deviation Road,' is all I can think to say. He asks if any of us are hurt. I shake my head. He seems stunned, speechless, in a state of disbelief. I tell him there's another large tree down just ahead, with a lot of cars piled into it. He looks at me strangely and inches the car on. An ambulance comes through behind it and then a CFA truck. 'This is the first lot in. They're cutting their way through,' I say to John. We feel shattered and plough on up Deviation Road.

Sean berates us when we arrive. He's still holding Carissa close and reassuring her, letting her drift in and out of sleep. 'That's the most dangerous thing you've done today. Everything is still exploding and falling. It's just not safe to be out there.' We relay the fact that an emergency crew has got through, describe the downed trees, the crashed cars, the houses still starting to burn, Lorrie and the stunned policeman. It occurs to us all that the roads must be blocked in every direction.

There is no desire to sleep. We're still going to have to wait. I have no idea what time it is, but I'm praying for dawn to break—to get rid of this interminable darkness, to be able to see what's around us. Brad and Mike are back outside, dousing the smouldering bases of the pine trees. Julie and I walk through the smoke to the end of the house that gives the best view towards the main road. There's a line of headlights coming down at a snail's pace. The beams are diffusing in the smoke, but we can make out flashing emergency lights. 'At least they're getting in,' Julie says.

I go back to the front lawn, lie down on a mattress and close my eyes. Harley comes and licks my face. He still doesn't want to stand for long and I try bathing his paws again, but he squeals and pulls away. His cough isn't getting any better either. I can't think of what else to do to relieve him except keep him quiet and still, so I pat and talk to him. We haven't begun to figure out what we are living through and what might lie ahead.

4

The day after

SUNDAY dawns; daylight is starting to come back now. There's also light from the diesel dump on the main road, which is still exploding and spewing fumes.

Sean heads back to Number 59 to check on the horses again. A short while later he's back. 'Come and help me over the road! The Smiths' sheds and woodpiles are starting to burn and we've got to get it away from our place,' he says. We race across, straight to the vegie garden, and Sean leaps the side fence and starts hurling burning firewood away. A small shed explodes. Sean arms himself with the shovel again and heaves out burning debris, hell-bent on saving this green oasis for the horses. Everything else is black and smouldering, as far as the eye can see.

Once Sean's satisfied that the fire's under control for now, we head back to Number 48. We have seen that the chimney is the only part of our house still standing; the rest is a pile of smoking rubble, just roofing iron lying on the ground. But daylight seems to have lifted everyone's morale and energy levels, and at least the others have had a bit of sleep.

The sound of a motorbike cuts through the air. Rose Chandler appears, dirt-biking up the blackened paddock. Go Rose! She dismounts. No words needed—they're alive, out of that hemmed-in spot at the bottom of the easement, which only has one exit. Their bushland is still burning and more is catching fire, she says, and trees are down. We walk with her to the front gate and see the look of horror on her face as she spots the fallen trees and burnt properties for the first time. 'Our house is gone,' I tell her. She can't comprehend it. She fills a container with drinking water from John and Julie's tank and heads back down the paddock.

Sarah is in kitchen-and-food-preparation mode with Julie— none of us has eaten since who knows when. Sean and John swing into practical action again, too. John is calculating how much petrol is left for the generator; he's been turning it on in a carefully devised pattern, trying to keep at least one fridge cold but also save enough fuel to power the water pump. With no mains power, we are totally reliant on this petrol-driven motor to run the vital electric pumps. We are also preserving mobile-phone batteries, as no one has a charger. The fuel tanks in our cars are still intact, so Brad and Mike decide to try to siphon the petrol from Sean's car and mine; for now, we'll leave John's with some in it, just in case we can get down the road. The duo head to Number 59 with fuel containers.

Another neighbour, Bernie Svoboda, arrives. His house has gone and his precious horses are badly burnt; he sought refuge with the Cahills. His wife Karen was away, off the mountain, when the fire happened and now she can't get near it. Bernie just sits with us. God knows when any vets will get in. 'Sorry, mate, my gun was inside the house,' Sean says, reflecting our unspoken accord about putting agonised animals out of their misery. Bernie asks about Ricky and Eliza. 'They're corralled in the vegie garden,' Sean says.

There's no conversation beyond that. Bernie heads back to the Cahills, and Sean and I go over to see how Brad and Mike are getting on with the petrol expedition. Carissa comes with us. She is speechless at the sight of the fallen mountain ash, and then she just stands and stares at the smoking ruins of the house. She clicks off endless photos, as if proving to herself that it has really gone. She walks over near the front shed and I notice pools of aluminium at the bottom of the Land Rover: the panels have melted and resolidified. 'It's a metre shorter than it used to be,' Sean says.

Carissa bends down and picks up something. It's a blackened bone-china teacup, the flower pattern still visible. She hands it to me. 'Put it in your pocket and keep it,' I tell her. 'That belonged to your great-great-grandmother. She was fond of afternoon tea parties.'

We hear a loud string of bad language coming from the other side of the driveway, most of it to do with the fact that our cars are refusing to let Brad and Mike into the fuel tanks. 'They're bloody burglar-proof,' Brad says. Just when you need a bit of siphoning, the manufacturers have come up with successful security systems!

Thwarted, we go back to Number 48 and John recalculates his generator running times. Julie is trying again to get onto Emergency Services, but now even the stalwart landline is buzzing in and out of connectedness. Out of the blue, my mobile rings. What's going on with these networks? It's my niece Amy in Tasmania: 'Aunty, we're watching these fires on TV and it's all about Kinglake. Are you okay?' I tell her we're all at John and Julie's, that I won't talk now, but can she please ring New Zealand and tell them we're alive, that Brad, Sarah and Mike are safe. My brother Carl and his wife will be frantic by now, not to mention Brad's sister Jo-Anna and her husband Chris. It's an enormous relief to be able to get any sort of message out.

Bernie comes back. His mobile is working, he has a phone charger in his car. Sean has a brainwave, borrows some of John's tools and heads off to his burnt car to extract the battery and the car-phone charger. He finds a wiring mechanism among John's gadgets and hooks it onto the battery terminals and starts charging his phone—he sits with the battery between his legs, trying to call the outside world. Bernie is breaking his heart over his horses; the rest of us feel helpless.

There's the sound of a car on the road, coming from the township end. A white dual-cab ute with CFA markings comes into view and roars down the easement towards the Chandlers'. Woo-hoo, the crews are coming in! A short time later, the ute returns and we wave it to a halt. Questions tumble out: 'What's going on? Is anybody getting off the mountain?' The poor guy is bombarded. There might be an evacuation bus going to Whittlesea later, he tells us, mostly women and children; the first priority is the injured. I ask if I can put Carissa's name down for the bus. 'If you've got people to go, get them to rally here in an hour or two. No guarantees that any vehicles will get in or out, though,' he says. The Cahills have also seen the CFA ute and their sons come across. We all exchange news, and we tell them about the possibility of getting out later in the afternoon. A CFA truck with a full crew swings into John and Julie's driveway and heads down the easement road to the Chandlers.

I tell Carissa there's a chance of her getting out on an evacuation bus. Sean has got through to Tania: she will go to Whittlesea and wait, she says, as they've set up a triage centre and evacuation point there. 'There's no guarantee they'll get out,' Sean tells her. 'We'll just keep trying to contact you and keep you posted.'

More waiting. I suggest to Brad, Sarah and Mike that they might be able to get on a bus as well, that Tania could get them back to the city and they can go home. They go away to discuss it.

'We're not going, Aunty,' Brad says when they return. 'Other people are of higher priority than us. We can be of much more use here, and we're all okay. We're not going.'

In the late afternoon, as the sun is starting to sink, the strike team appears again. They pull over next to the carport. 'We'll take your granddaughter and any others down to the CFA station,' the team leader tells us. 'Don't know how long they'll have to wait there,' he adds.

The Cahill brothers, Robert and Alan, bring their sister and her partner and baby boy across. The strike-team captain approaches me: 'I can't really describe what they're going to see when they go down that mountain. It's horrific. Are you okay with that?' But I'd rather have Carissa back with her mother, not breathing in this toxic smoke, safe in her own bed. She climbs onto the back of the truck and they put a red blanket around her. She's still taking photos. I give the crew Tania's mobile number and ask Robert Cahill if he'll stay with Carissa on the way down, make sure she connects at the other end. He says he will. They climb on and I want to cry as the truck heads out of sight. I'm torn between wanting to protect her from any further horror and getting her to safety. I know she has to get off this mountain if she can, and I have to accept that I can't shield her from whatever she comes across on the way.

Another truck, a crew from Wattle Glen, has pulled into the roadway and they're firing water at the base of John and Julie's pine trees. Trying to damp things down, keep the sparks and embers under control. They're homing in on the houses that are still standing, to make sure they stay that way. I race to the back fence and ask one of the crew if he's got a burns kit in the truck. 'Is one of you injured? I'll call for help,' he says. 'No, it's my dog. He's burnt his paws badly and I just need to get them bandaged,' I say. 'No problem. I can handle animals as well as humans,' says this smiling young man. He walks down the lawn with the first-aid kit and kneels beside Harley, who isn't walking at all now. The young man talks to him—soothing, kind—applies thick pads and then bandages the front paws. 'You realise that you'll have to get me onto *Bondi Vet* after this,' he jokes. I want to hug him or at least send a nice note to his parents telling them they've raised a gem.

The crew leaves, telling us to call the CFA if there's any outbreak of embers. They are still hosing the bases of the trees as they go. Julie and I retreat back to the front lawn. I feel comforted that Carissa has a chance of getting out and Harley has some respite from pain. John and Sean continue their patrolling. Sean's mobile phone is going crazy with an endless stream of messages and frantic texts from friends, family and old acquaintances. He can read them, but can't reply. 'What's being said about us in the outside world?' he muses.

A loud voice breaks into our reverie. 'Oh my God, you're alive!' Hurtling through the gate is John Duthie, a friend who lives with wife Maddie and their two little daughters on the other side of the township. He claps his hands to his head. 'I've just been past Number 59. The cars are burnt in the driveway and the house is gone. I thought you must be dead,' he says. He had sunk to his knees in our driveway, he tells us, until Greek John happened on him. 'I kept saying to him, "Where are the O'Connors?"' 'They're over the road on the front lawn,' John replied. There's a group hug: me, Sean and John Duthie in a big, fierce embrace.

John Duthie falls in a heap on the lawn. He tells us that news of multiple deaths is filtering through in the township. A lot of houses have gone down there; the ridge roads at the back of us, which run off the main road, have been particularly badly hit. John and Maddie's close friends the Daveys are believed to be dead, along with their two little girls, the same age as the Duthies'. We are silent: this is incomprehensible, too much to deal with.

John heads back to tell Maddie we're alive. Sean and I walk up to the front gate, just trying to get our thoughts together. We see Mark Smith walking through the front of his property, coming towards us, kicking up blackened dirt with his boots. He too has his hands on top of his head. He slides down the embankment onto the road, flopping down on the bitumen. 'Oh Christ, oh Christ,' is all he can say. His eyes are filled with tears and he lets out a primal sob: 'My best mate's kids have burnt to death. Oh Christ!'

We're shocked rigid. 'We're all okay, though,' Mark says. 'Kevin got the other two to Yea. He had to drive through fireballs, but he made it—God knows how he didn't crash into something. I saw your tenants. They were standing in the driveway, terrified. Dionne and I yelled at them to head for the pub and they left in their car. We don't know if they made it, but they headed that way,' he adds. 'Whose kids are dead?' I ask. 'The Buchanans' kids, Macca and Neeve.' It's my turn for a primal sob: Neeve, the cheeky little blonde friend of Kelsey's. Just two weeks ago they rode their bikes across to Julie's for biscuits and milk and then did the circuit to Number 59, where we set them up with a bag of lollies, a plate of ice-cream and *Willy Wonka* on our big-screen TV. I'm seeing that smiling little face, rerunning the banter, too numb to cry.

Mark feels satisfied that we're all safe and heads back to his family. Sean and I are silent. How the hell do you take that in?

Back at Number 48 we find Rose Chandler there again. I tell her about the Buchanan kids. She puts her hands over her ears. 'Too much, too much,' she says. Sarah and Julie are inside making a tuna salad. They've chopped red onion, rustled up mayonnaise and found a lettuce. Suddenly, food seems like a good idea; I feel ravenous and realise we haven't eaten since yesterday morning. 'That's a bit flash under the circumstances,' I say, but admire their resourcefulness. We take the salad outside on the lawn.

Julie notices there are buses heading up the main road. 'Looks like they *are* evacuating people. Carissa is on her way out,' she says. My stomach lurches and I know it will stay knotted until I hear she is safe.

We stand there and wave, just in case Carissa's looking. The bus lights are muted in the ever-present smoke. It's been one hell of a Sunday.

Sleep remains elusive, in spite of our overwhelming sense of relief that Carissa has made it off the mountain. Tania gets the message through that she's home safe, exhausted and in bed. Our mobile phones are still warping in and out of the network; the bombardment of messages whenever we turn them on continues to be overwhelming.

We decide to devote some generator time to the 7 p.m. ABC news. Watching it is a surreal experience. Over the years, I've written plenty of headlines and churned out running copy on disasters and major events, but never imagined being the subject of that sort of news commentary. There it all is: mounting death tolls, emergency crews, communities cut off, the injured being evacuated, roadblocks in place; Strathewen decimated, Marysville gone, Steel's Creek scorched, killer fires in Gippsland, flames close to Bendigo. Full-alert fire threats are still being broadcast. It's too much to process all at once—too close to home, too personal—and we can only absorb it in short grabs. We have no comprehension at this stage of exactly where the fire we're still battling has come from. One thing we all loudly agree, though, is that there was no warning, that we were already burning well before Kinglake was first mentioned. We feel angry and abandoned. 'How could they not have seen a firestorm like that coming?' Sean asks, incredulous.

Julie's habit of a lifetime is to record, review and rework; she has a chronicler's mind. Tonight she is adamant about what she has heard and noted. 'We had to make our own decision to get going. If Ken hadn't come by and talked about what he was seeing in that smoke cloud, we wouldn't have even got this far,' she says. We don't watch the entire news bulletin—we know only too well what we're in the middle of. That people are dead has come as no surprise, given what John and I saw on the main road last night. What we can't fathom is the scale of it.

'People have panicked and got in their cars,' Sean says. 'That's what Carissa and I saw on the powerline road. They were streaming up there or trying to get down. Most of them wouldn't be able to deal with the steepness and gravel.' Then he adds, 'Oh God, I hope the Strathewen hall is okay.' That hall has been a favourite venue for years. On Sundays Sean would load his drum kit into the Land Rover and head down there for a jam session with his brother Marty and other members of their blues band. And we've held birthdays there.

Our ember patrols continue for the rest of the night, more emergency crews crawl down the main road, our mobile phones regularly beep message signals. We all hunker down again to get through to morning. Darkness is hell: we're too pumped with adrenaline, too agitated and too restless to sleep. We count down to dawn.

5

The longest week

WHEN Monday's morning light arrived, nothing had changed. The pine trees were still smouldering, the road still blocked. Sean continued to check on the goats and horses. Harley was distressed and in obvious pain, with blood oozing through the bandages on his front paws, and he lay on his stomach holding them up off the ground. The tail still wagged, though. His hacking cough continued and I was totally agitated, wanting to take away his pain. 'He was pretty amazing. He was stomping on the fire with his paws when he got over here, barking when new bits burst into flames,' John told me. 'He wouldn't let up until I'd put them out.'

I suggested to Sean that we walk to the other end of Deviation Road to see if Kate and Ivan Rowbotham were there. We had no idea if their house was still standing. Ivan is a highly trained first-aider and a member of Kinglake's first-response ambulance crew: he was bound to have some serious burns preparations and bandages. It was worth a try, so we headed off past Number 59, past the Cahills'. Their house was still there, but everything else was razed—sheds, fences, tanks, trees. We continued around the bend and up past Karen and Bernie's: nothing left, not even a blade of grass. The Mitchells' mudbrick house had been blown apart as if a missile had sliced through it, and its surrounding stand of old mountain ash was decimated.

The entire left-hand side of the road was a black, smoking mess, no structures left standing. The right-hand side was a bomb site. We were flabbergasted: the trees weren't just burnt, they'd had the life sucked out of them. Fences had vanished, even the white lines in the middle of the road had melted away. We punched on towards Kate and Ivan's. We were walking through a disaster movie; I felt cold. The Lawlesses' house was still there—nothing else, just the house.

Kate and Ivan's house and sheds loomed up in front of us where Deviation Road rejoins the main road. So too did the next shock: sitting in the intersection was a car on its side, and a further six were resting where they had landed in the middle of the road. They'd either hit head-on, or rear-ended the vehicle in front. A fatal demolition derby. A BMW was lying on its side, the paint stripped off it—no colour left, just the shape and badge identified it. Police ribbons fluttered off door handles. Both ends of our road were cluttered with scenes of human horror.

'Jesus, nobody would have been able to see a thing in the smoke,' Sean said, his voice echoing in an eerie way. The surrounding silence was palpable; it was a scene frozen in time—it had happened while we were fighting for our own survival. We had no ghoulish desire to go any closer. The emergency crews would have had to pick their way through this to get to the township: they knew it was here.

We headed down Kate and Ivan's driveway. They answered the door and ushered us in. We were thrilled to see each other, to know we were all alive. They hadn't left the house since Saturday night. I burbled about how I'd come to get bandages and burn cream for Harley. We swapped stories about what had hit us and how we'd got through the firestorm. Ivan put the kettle on: a hot cup of tea—what bliss. Their gas bottles had survived, though all the PVC water pipes and tanks had come off second-best. We were amazed that they had fared pretty well given they were in a heavily treed area, right in the path of the fires that had been propelled up the slope by the south-west wind change. Fire can be an indiscriminate beast.

We talked about the lack of warning before the fire. Ivan was used to being on emergency alert, as part of the ambulance service. 'Once we realised what was coming towards us, when we saw that column of smoke, we went out to the shed to put our fire gear on,' he said. 'In the time it took to get from the house into the shed, the fire had hit and we were trapped in there.' Their beloved dog Anna had followed them. They'd crawled under a workbench as the terrible heat seared through the metal of the structure. 'I haven't got a clue how long we were there,' continued Ivan. 'The flames were coming in under the roof. It was a toss-up whether the radiant heat or the smoke would get us first.' Kate described how he lay on top of her, shielding her, urging her to breathe. We joked about men never missing an opportunity. It was good to have a laugh.

Until they could escape the shed and get back into the house, Kate and Ivan were unaware of the destruction and horror occurring just metres away on the intersection. The fire noise drowned out everything. They'd been living in the midst of a landscape of panic and death since dawn broke on Sunday—you can't drown that out. At least they knew that the Lawlesses, next door, had survived: Craig had suffered burns while fighting to save the house and keep his parents safe, but they were all alive. We walked back to Number 48. It was impossible to describe to the others what we'd seen. It came out in bursts—the cars, the devastation, who had survived. God, we were ticking off a list of our neighbours.

Sean and I went across to Number 59. It was the first time I'd had a close look—for the past two days I'd skirted the house area, heading straight for the animals. This one was a slow journey. The driveway remained blocked by the tangled trees and bent front gates. There were gouges in the red gravel, caused by the deluge released from water tanks as they melted. The Land Rover was crushed under the carport roof, its melted windscreen wrapped around the skeletal steering column.

'What sort of heat can do that?' I asked Sean.

'Hot enough to melt aluminium,' he replied. 'Not to mention my drum kit.' The loss of the drum kit stung.

Our other cars in the driveway were equally wrecked. We decided to see if we could retrieve CDs and whatever else was in them. The rest of the trip was an obstacle course: we had to pick our way across the roof iron and up the side brick path to get further onto the property. There was shattered glass everywhere; the disintegrated house crumbled to dust as we walked over it. 'So much for the theory about non-native plants being fire-retardants,' Sean said. The entire garden, particularly at the front, was stripped bare: established camellias and rhododrendrons, large stands of hydrangeas, European trees, Norwegian spruce—all gone. The denser, greener, less oily characteristics of European flora are supposed to render them more fire-resistant. 'If that fire melted cars,' offered Sean, 'it could burn anything.' Then, in the backyard, we stopped dead in our tracks and laughed. The stainless-steel barbecue had survived, not a scratch on it, and the enclosed gas bottle seemed to be intact as well. Great! If it worked, we'd be able to have a hot meal and boil some water. The cheap, glass-topped outdoor table had made it as well, despite having been picked up and blown into the vegie garden area, where it now lay.

Sean was still upset about his inability to save the house and kept analysing what went wrong. 'Nothing went wrong,' I told him. 'There was no plan that could have coped with what hit us.' On the side lawn, he started to laugh. Standing under the sycamore tree was our old deck table, which we'd parked there after Sean had built a fabulous new one from recycled timber. The new one had gone up in flames; the veteran, with its bowed legs and fifteen years of use, hadn't been touched.

'I'm going to sift through the rubble later. Some things might have survived and your jewellery might still be okay,' Sean said. I wasn't hopeful and anyway, at this point, material things seemed utterly irrelevant. We decided to walk down the road and check out Number 1. The only remnants were the chimney, a small cast-iron potbelly stove, and the Hills hoist standing at a crazy angle. As we'd seen earlier, the tenants' pet goats lay blackened, belly-up. 'They must have had them tethered on the lawn,' said Sean.

Suddenly, the ground seemed to be shifting beneath us. We looked down: we were standing on a carpet of seething maggots—bloated white maggots. Clearly, the blowflies had come in for a breeding frenzy. 'We'd better try and bury the goats as quickly as possible,' I said. There must be dead livestock all over the mountain; the thought of a blowfly invasion filled me with dread.

We left that task for later and instead wheeled the barbecue back from Number 59, feeling like a couple of kids who had scored a major prize. The looks on the faces of the others was worth a thousand words. The barbecue fired up first time, water went on the wok burner and we all engaged in watched-pot syndrome. How long the gas would last was another matter, but for now we were coveting a hot drink and a cooked meal. The men collected our outdoor table and chairs, and set them up on the front lawn.

The vinyl covers were pocked with burn marks and holes, but they were usable.

Time had ceased to have any meaning; we were on some sort of autopilot. Clock watching wasn't a consideration, as there were no specific mealtimes or routines in place. I was still conscious of what we were ingesting: our lungs hurt and our eyes were dry and painful. The mountain had turned strangely cold again. Nobody had slept since Friday night, more than forty-eight hours ago, but there was no sense of needing to. There was a crazy, collective momentum.

Tania called. She was putting some essential supplies together for us and was canvassing all the delivery drivers at Whittlesea to try to get the stuff up the mountain. 'Nobody's getting through the roadblocks, only emergency supplies,' she said. 'I've told them I have to get medical supplies up there. Sean's Ventolin, and has John got enough insulin? What else should I put on board? And by the way, they're talking about sending the army in.' I told her about the barbecue and can't remember what else I asked her to try to get on a truck, other than Sean's blood-pressure medication.

Our main news was now coming from Tania or via the bush telegraph. We weren't getting anything immediately useful from radio or television, which were still breathlessly covering the mounting death toll and ongoing fire alerts. John Duthie came back to check on us and insisted we take his second car. 'Some people have travelled off the mountain, but from all reports it's pretty horrendous,' he said. 'And if they go through the roadblocks then they can't get back up again.' The idea of borrowing somebody else's car challenged us, as we'd never had to do that before. But John wouldn't take no for an answer and we knew we might need to get down to the township or go to Whittlesea because there was already talk of a community meeting the next day and of trucks bringing supplies. John and Julie's cars were low on fuel; one was diesel and we'd agreed to keep the other's petrol for the generator.

'I'll go to town tomorrow to see if any more evacuation buses are going,' I told Julie. 'If they are, we'll get Sarah, Brad and Mike on one. They've got a very long trip home.' Brad was still reluctant to move, though, feeling he was of more use here. They had contacted their employers in New Zealand, who had swung into action to organise any accommodation, replacement clothes and food they might need. John was delighted with Tania's news that the army might be coming in. He'd talked about this the night before. 'Put the army on the roadblocks. Call them in to clear the roads. And they've got some of the best firefighting gear in the business,' he said again now.

On Tuesday morning, Julie and I headed into Kinglake. The crashed cars were still littering the main road, but some of the fallen trees had been bulldozed to the side. In the township, dozens of cars were still parked near the CFA station and people were milling about, dazed and disoriented, many looking as though they'd slept there. We went to the police station and I explained to the senior officer behind the counter, 'I've got three New Zealanders who need to get off the mountain. Are any evacuation buses going out today? They need replacement documents, so can anybody get in touch with their consul?' The words sounded inane in the light of what was happening all around us. He smiled, then explained that evacuations were a bit hit-and-miss at the moment because the roads were unstable and dangerous; the crews were trying to remove any trees that were likely to fall. 'Tell you what, since the poor old Kiwis suffered enough at the cricket, I'll take them to Whittlesea. I'm finishing my shift in half an hour,' he said.

What came out of my mouth next was involuntary. 'I don't suppose you've got room for a large dog? He's badly burnt and his temperature is up. He isn't going to make it if he doesn't get to a vet. My daughter will meet you in Whittlesea and take him. He's a black labrador.' He smiled again. 'I reckon we can find room for a big, smelly woofer. I'd be pretty happy to see anything survive up here at the moment. Have them ready and back here in half an hour.' This came with the same warning as before: 'It won't be pretty on the way down. It's fairly horrendous and it'll be a slow trip.'

Julie and I just about broke the land speed record as we raced back to Deviation Road. But as we came up the main road we were waved over by a CFA crew, who were still damping down the smouldering ruins of the nursery café and its garden. The tall fireman looked distressed. 'We've got to move on, but there's a cat with new kittens in the glasshouse,' he said. 'We haven't got anywhere to take them and we're worried in case she hasn't got food. We've put some water in there, though.' There were tears in his eyes. Most of the firefighters we'd come across so far had been like this: shell-shocked, disbelieving, up for a spontaneous hug on sighting survivors. We pledged to take some food down later. The fireman and his female colleague were enormously relieved—nobody had been able to get in for animals yet.

Back at Number 48, we didn't give the New Zealand trio a choice—they were to get out now, to safety. Sean drove them back to the police station while I alerted Tania to their impending arrival. She stationed herself at Whittlesea again and continued to approach the delivery drivers. Hours went by before she was in touch again: Brad, Sarah and Mike were at home with her, and Harley was in intensive care with the local vet, his paws being tended to under anaesthetic. She said Harley was close to meltdown by the time they carried him in, and it was going to be a long haul. If he pulled out of the anaesthetic, he was up for painstaking daily treatment. 'Mind you, even as they were putting him under the tail didn't stop wagging,' said Tania. You can't keep a good labrador down. 'But you might have warned me about that cop! There's me in the tracksuit pants and ponytail, and this gorgeous sort gets out of the car with the dog,' she joked. She had also found a delivery driver willing to bring two cartons up the mountain the next day and would take them to him in the morning.

'He doesn't know what time he'll get there,' said Tania. 'They're all saying it's a case of inch-by-inch up the mountain, because they're trying to clear roads. I'll call you when he's leaving, so he can meet you somewhere.' I was blown away by her tenacity.

For the first time in days, I fell in a heap. All I wanted was a wash. We got the barbecue going again to heat up a big pot of water, so we could all at least freshen up a bit. It was the first time in four days that I'd taken my boots off and they'd just about stuck to my feet. Sean held up his Blundstones: the soles were melted, no tread left. His padded woollen shirt was full of holes where embers had hit—you could see daylight through them. It was the first time we'd noticed.

The Chandlers called by and they too had heard news of a community meeting and some supplies getting in. So, on Wednesday morning we headed for town. Julie stayed behind, as conditions were still too volatile to leave the property unattended. In Kinglake, emergency-services caravans had been set up near the shire offices. People were again standing about aimlessly. There were some we recognised and others whose faces were familiar but who we didn't know personally. They hugged us anyway—simply acknowledging that we were all in the same boat. I spotted Michelle, the former pub landlady I'd done kitchen duty with during the 2006 fires. 'A bit different to last time, mate,' she said. Everybody was swapping notes about whose house had survived and whose hadn't. A woman I'd never met before walked towards me, sobbing, devastated that her house was intact and ours had gone. In the middle of this bizarre scene, she kept apologising. I told her it was okay, that anything that had survived was to be celebrated. Survivor guilt had started early.

Tania called to say that the delivery guy would be pulling in near the CFA station: the boxes would have our name on them. She told us she'd given him Sean's mobile number and she gave us the driver's name and the truck's registration number. She'd pulled it off! While we hovered around there waiting, I spotted our local vet, Dr Kate Murray—always an integral part of our community—who was treating animals out of the boot of her car, on a makeshift table.

I walked towards her and we hugged. The surgery had been destroyed, she told me, and all she could do for now was deal with the worst cases. People were bringing dogs that had been left behind or confined to backyards at the height of the firestorm, or had fled in terror. For now she was gathering them together for transport off the mountain, and she was expecting the RSPCA to get in soon with stockfeed, more vets, and drug supplies. This must be the toughest gig a vet could ever face—pure triage. She said the Whittlesea vet was prepared for the emergency cases when she could ship them out. I told her that Harley had gone to Eltham. 'Did you warn them that he can wreck a vet's surgery with that tail?' Kate asked. She hadn't lost her sense of humour.

We spotted Tania's truck coming in and collared the driver as soon as he pulled over. He pointed to cartons with our name on them and we stashed them in the car. Now was not the time to make it known that we'd managed to get supplies through the roadblocks. Unpacking the boxes could wait.

Slowly, the people who had stayed or were trapped on the mountain started heading towards the shire offices. Some had lost friends and neighbours, and their pain was raw. A barbecue was happening for those who needed hot food, and drinking water was available. It was cold and I was once again grateful for the Tibetan jacket. We spotted more friends and acquaintances in the crowd and hugged, silently—there weren't any words to say at a time like this. Trauma counsellors and church chaplains were mingling with the people, not intruding, just letting you know they were there. Maddie Duthie sidled over to me with her little girls, slipped her hand into mine and squeezed it; we choked back the tears. Her three-year-old was happily playing with a bird feather she'd picked up off the ground—smiling and chattering. We didn't want to break the mood, so I picked up the 'news' in grabs.

Some people were angry and demanding. They couldn't get back through the roadblocks if they went off the mountain; some had children elsewhere and wanted them to come back. ('Why would you want your children back in this environment?' a council official asked.) Others were insisting that generators be brought in to provide power for houses that had survived; some wanted fuel, despite the fact that the chances of being allowed to bring fuel into a still-active fire area were zero. There were complaints about having had no hot food for days, and still no phone access. The police attempted to calm everyone down. They were working on a system through the roadblocks, with car stickers to identify locals, they told us, but for now they couldn't allow open-slather access for friends and relatives—the roads were, after all, not only dangerous but also now a death scene, awaiting the coroner's attention.

Centrelink and the State Department of Human Services had set up in the council offices and were urging everybody to register for emergency grants: cash payments would be made immediately, with further funds available once paperwork was completed. I found this mildly ludicrous—there wasn't much to spend money on here. Telstra had also brought in an emergency crew, who were setting up wireless internet access and had mobile-phone chargers—the latter interested me more. Some clothing and food supplies were being organised in the café.

We were herded towards the council offices and asked to stand in line to register. I assumed this was linked to the Red Cross's efforts to trace people listed as missing. Sean had no identification, his wallet now reduced to ashes on the kitchen bench. We did as asked and stood in the queue: more familiar faces, more stories to swap, more tears and trauma. Finally our turn came and we sat at a desk, total strangers to accessing any sort of government services and somehow feeling embarrassed and undeserving. All I recall is giving details automatically and being handed money. I decided to leave registering with Centrelink for another day, until I noticed a department official using a mobile phone the same as mine. My trip to the pub revealed that Telstra had run out of my brand, so I asked her if she had a charger. She shepherded me into the caravan and I plugged in my phone, then headed to the café to see if there was a change of clothes available.

Maddie Duthie was already at the café, helping make up clothing packages. It was chaos, as the speed with which the first aid shipments had been packed was posing an urgent sorting problem. But locals had joined with emergency workers to get on with the job, and this sweet-natured young woman was unpacking cartons and trying to create some order. 'Let me know what you need the most and I'll make you up a pile,' she said. I really hadn't got a clue. 'Some undies would be good, if any come in. And shoes. Anything, I don't care, just shoes so I can get rid of these boots,' I said. I left without anything at this point, as my brain simply couldn't fathom picking over the clothing piles or taking things in the hope that they might fit.

I headed back to retrieve my phone. The Centrelink rep asked if I'd registered. 'Can't quite get my head around all this,' I replied. 'Let me guess,' she said. 'You've never been to Centrelink in your life. But I'll bet you've always paid your taxes. Well, you are now deservedly receiving some of those taxes; this is your money. It's people like you that concern us the most, because you don't want to claim these things. Believe me, you are going to need every cent of it. So, sit down and I'll fill out the form for you.'

It still felt odd. The entire process had been strangely exhausting, and it was not possible to comprehend fully that we were homeless refugees, that we owned only what we were standing up in. There hadn't been any opportunity to calculate insurance or worry about mortgage payments or even think of finances—the adrenaline-charged brain inhabits a different universe. I detoured back via the temporary Telstra set-up, where the technicians took my recharged phone and diverted our home number to it just in case anybody was trying to contact us that way.

Sean, John and I headed back to Julie with Tania's survival cartons. Somehow, my daughter had even got a jerrycan of fuel on board. 'That girl is amazing,' John exclaimed. 'And just when we're down to the last of ours.' We ripped the cartons open: one revealed changes of clothes for me, plus sneakers, underwear, pants, tops, a warm jacket, Sean's medications and, lurking down the bottom, a couple of bottles of wine, a carton of cigarettes, a large bottle of Diet Coke for John and a block of dark chocolate. She'd covered everybody. The other box contained fresh fruit and vegetables for us and a swag of carrots and greens for the horses and goats.

We called Tania, who said she was already working on the next load. I suggested she hold off for the moment because we were planning to go to Whittlesea the next day. (There was talk that the authorities were issuing temporary ID wristbands—the bush telegraph was outdoing the news bulletins again.) But Tania had found someone else coming in that afternoon and they would drop off gas bottles to keep the precious barbecue going.

Tania swung her attention to finding agistment for the horses and a temporary home for the goats. And just as well—when Sean went across to feed them later that afternoon he discovered they'd gone and saw a horse float heading off the property. He stopped them and it turned out that they were animal-welfare volunteers who had simply walked onto our place and loaded them up. 'Where were you planning to take them and when were you going to tell us?' Sean asked. 'We were going to leave a note in the letterbox,' they said. What letterbox? There wasn't one left in our road. Sean diverted them to the temporary grazing that had been set up in a spot spared by the fire. We seemed ungrateful, perhaps, but we felt assaulted and invaded. This was the first of many well-meaning actions by people with their hearts in the right place but their heads not necessarily thinking in a sensible direction. Kate Murray had assured us the RSPCA was mobilising its forces and we felt more secure with official bodies than unknown groups.

That night was the first time we contemplated any sort of future action. 'You stay here for as long as it takes. There's plenty of room and it just isn't an issue,' John said. He's not a man who says something he doesn't mean. Tania was equally keen that we stay with her for a few days, just to sort our heads out—we couldn't finish sentences or hold a thought, let alone come to any rational conclusions.

Personal safety was also becoming an issue. We felt alarmed over the horses being taken, and John and Julie were on their own at our end of the road. There were a dozen ways—dirt tracks, fire trails—onto the mountain apart from the main roads: the locals knew them and it was only a matter of time before opportunists discovered them. Disasters bring out the very best in people, but also the very worst, and I'd seen enough of them to know that scavengers and looters were quick off the mark. To suggest that such actions wouldn't occur in a civilised society was delusional— we all knew that and were on standby. A key target would be the surviving properties whose owners were either away on the day of the fire or had subsequently left, traumatised. John wasn't going to leave his property.

Our attention was distracted when Sean came in with a baby possum he'd found sitting on the driveway. It had clung to his arm when he picked it up, and in shock had sunk its teeth into his neck. It was badly burnt and unlikely to survive, but we gave it a try. The poor little creature, with its blistered face and raw paws and tail, slurped sugar water from one of John's insulin syringes. It could hardly breathe, but at least had some hydration. Julie and I cut the toe out of an old work sock and let the possum crawl in there; it died overnight.

There was no such thing as sleeping through the night at this point. We'd snatch a few hours, wander about, keep an eye on smouldering trees and then doze a bit more. 'We've reverted to the old farming days. Going to bed on dark and getting up at dawn,' Julie said. It was programmed into our body clocks.

Early on Thursday morning, Sean and I headed for Whittlesea. Tania was going to meet us there. At the junction of Deviation Road and the main road a police car with lights flashing was diverting the supply trucks around the wrecks. Skirting these, we slowly headed beyond Kinglake for Pheasant Creek, about 5 kilometres to the west, noting the houses that had gone, more head-on collisions and cars run into banks, dead animals, smoking flora and power poles littering the verges. One horse lay on its side, bloated, crashed into a front fence. Water tanks stood half melted and twisted, pastures were blackened, pine plantations reduced to airy twigs. There was no rhyme or reason to what had survived and what hadn't: houses in the middle of cleared ground had gone, while others surrounded by dense bush were still standing. 'It must have depended on where the fireballs hit and how the wind went,' Sean said. Rough, hand-painted signs had already gone up on some properties, warning looters they would be shot.

Just beyond Pheasant Creek we came into a green zone—a tract of land untouched, not a scorch mark on it. But at the intersection with the Whittlesea–Yea Road it turned to overwhelming destruction again. We inched between the stop signs, past black earth and road signs melted like candle wax. Crews were up still-smouldering trees, working feverishly to clear debris. 'That's a hell of a job,' Sean said. We passed Coombs Road, an enclave we'd often admired but where we could now see for miles through the stripped trees. We'd earlier caught some news suggesting that people had died here, including the former television newsreader Brian Naylor. His son Matt had for years cut our hay and done our fencing, and we'd felt gutted when he was killed in an ultralight-plane accident a year ago. There was just too much information to keep absorbing, as a trip that would normally take around thirty-five minutes turned into an hour and a half. Mount Disappointment loomed on our right—it was charcoal. At the bottom of the mountain we came across the first police roadblock. At least I had my driver's licence showing our address: they assured us we could return, as we'd be issued with wristbands.

The relief centre was set up near the Whittlesea shire offices. The showgrounds had been turned into a medical triage centre and fire-truck rallying point. We were ushered into a parking area and directed straight to the Red Cross facility. It was one of the strangest experiences of our lives, being sat at a desk to register the fact that we were alive. I've long admired Red Cross officials working under horrendous circumstances in other countries and now here we were, on the receiving end.

Lying on the desk was one of those little knitted bears, a cuddly toy they hand out to children in traumatic situations. I found myself picking it up. 'Don't mind me,' I said to the woman behind the desk. She just smiled: 'That's what they're there for.' I filled out the form and asked if I could check to see if others we knew had registered as safe, reeling off the names of neighbours and friends. She plugged them into a computer. 'There are a lot of people looking for you and Sean. They've listed you as missing,' she said. Many of them were people we'd been unable to contact on the sporadic mobile network.

Our neighbours and the tenants from Number 1 came up as alive. How utterly bloody odd, I thought, sitting here ticking off who's dead and who's alive. Then I felt arms going around me, from behind, hugging me like there was no tomorrow. It was Tania, crushing me to death, shaking. It was the first time I'd cried. 'Let's get outside,' I said. The hovering trauma counsellors followed us: reunion scenes like this must have been very common over the past few days and they were ready to catch us if we imploded. Sean had gone off to try to replace his driver's licence. 'I feel naked without any ID at all,' he said.

Tania and I retreated to the small tent they'd set up to allow people some privacy. They brought us coffee and left us alone. Tears turned to a chuckle when Tania and I agreed we really weren't 'counselling' sort of people; we'd effectively told them to bugger off. Other people were clinging to the case-workers like a lifeline—different people react in different ways. We returned to the Red Cross centre to finish the paperwork and were diverted across to the Salvation Army. They handed us money. 'You're going to need it,' they said. I wanted to run screaming, I felt like a thief—others needed this more than I did—but these people, having had years of practice in such situations, seemed to detect the horrified reticence and left us with no choice.

Suddenly I was hungry, my stomach naggingly empty. Sean, Tania and I headed for the sausage sizzle. There was nowhere to sit, so we hung over a rubbish bin and scoffed comforting sausages in bread. A material-aid centre had been set up. Sean was desperately in need of clothes, but the volunteers there were apologetic: goods were pouring in by the truckload but, as in Kinglake, they still had to be unpacked and sorted. We were feeling overwhelmed by all the activity around us. 'The whole country has mobilised,' said Tania. 'They're raising huge amounts of money already.' It left us speechless—the O'Connors were more used to giving to charity than receiving it—but for now there was little choice.

Even the simple act of having to decide what clothes we needed turned into a muddle of indecision, which I again put down to ongoing adrenaline overload. But we snapped back to autopilot and selected some practical stuff: I was keen to find some things for Carissa, as half her clothes as well as jewellery, her handbag and all her new school gear had been at Number 59. Choosing replacement items for her was easy, but when I looked at the piles of clothes I just couldn't relate them to myself. Tania took charge again and we reversed roles. She'd select things and hold them up. I'd reject them, but she'd put them in a bag anyway, figuring that plain T-shirts, a few more undies and socks would be gratefully received at a less manic moment. The only thing I grabbed for myself was a pair of tracksuit pants—fluoro mauve, made for teenagers and surf chicks, overpriced in the shops and emblazoned with a designer name.

'Lucky I've never been a slave to fashion,' I said to Tania.

Sean gathered up basic tops and pants, socks and underwear. I was still obsessed about finding a pair of shoes. Nothing here, but it was suggested that some would be coming in at the weekend. 'Let's head down the road and we'll get you some more basics at Kmart or Target,' Tania said. I was happy to let her take charge. I was like a kid being taken shopping for school gear—it had to happen, but none of it was exciting.

Walking into a shopping centre was really challenging. I felt like a freak. Everybody was bound to be looking at us—dirty, dishevelled, hair a mess, red eyes, no make-up, and ready to either cry or scream at the drop of a hat, especially if anybody spoke to me. I was emotionally numb and it was difficult to handle people's reactions when they realised we'd come from Kinglake. All I wanted to do was get a pair of black pants, a white shirt and basic black shoes—enough to go to work in—and then get out of there. I'd decided to go back to work the following Monday, head for some routine and normality, or at least try to. Shoes remained elusive, as I couldn't bring myself to buy some just for the sake of it, if they weren't comfortable. I couldn't face trawling around other shops and, anyway, nobody at work would worry about the fact that I was wearing my daughter's sneakers with a pair of Kmart pants.

We headed back to the mountain, filling up with petrol on the way. Tania was concerned about Carissa and returned to Eltham. Carissa had been quiet and withdrawn since the fire and had suffered the additional blow of losing school friends, who'd been burnt to death while on a sleepover. Her survivor guilt was working overtime, though she had access to good services if she needed them; she, too, was finding it difficult to deal with the overwhelming sympathy from others. 'Tell her we've all got to start thinking like survivors rather than victims,' I said. Tania was also tending to Harley, who was on strong sedatives to keep him quiet. 'His eyes were rolling around in his head, but the tail was still thumping. They might have to surgically separate the pads on his

paws because they look like fusing together,' said Tania. We told
her to assure the vet that cost wasn't an issue, that they should just
do whatever it took to get him through.

The drive back to Deviation Road was tiring, both physically
and mentally. Just dealing with the practical issues had left us wrung
out. We got our temporary wristbands at the roadblock and felt
like inmates, but they gave us a great sense of security: the thought
of unauthorised people invading the mountain was chilling. Leave
us be, we were all thinking, let us deal with what we have to deal
with in peace; we didn't want to be treated like a curiosity, a tourist
attraction. Police were arguing with the drivers of the cars stopped
in front of us, and swiftly turned them around. Unbelievably, some
were trying to get in for a close-up look at human misery and loss
while it was still raw and bleeding. Others were friends or family
with supplies but it was no go for them too.

Soon after we arrived back at Number 48, an RSPCA van
pulled in. They were checking surviving properties to see who
needed help with animals. There were dog treats for Meg and Jazz,
supplies of pet food, and a large bag of seed for the native birds.
In fact, we hadn't seen or heard birds for days, though there were
plenty of dead ones littering what had been our lawn—they'd
simply dropped out of the sky in the heat, flames and smoke. But
we left seed out for any survivors and a bale of hay for the resident
wombats and wallabies, of which, the RSPCA inspector indicated,
they were finding more dead than alive.

We gave her the address of the place where the horses had gone and she pledged to send the vets there to check them over. Hay had been dropped to the goats and we were now waiting for them to be picked up and taken temporarily off the mountain. Julie had got in touch with local goat-breeders who, despite having lost one of their group in the fire, had joined forces to help others, concerned about the lack of fences and the chance of animals wandering onto roads. The RSPCA inspector called back again later to tell us the horses had had their burnt legs treated and that Ricky had gashes from barbed wire, but they were okay.

The world around us was still hazy with smoke and ash. We could hear dogs howling in the distance as dusk descended, and the inspector headed off to see if she could locate the source of the mournful sounds. This was incredibly soothing, as I'd been hearing that sorrowful, abandoned baying for days. An insurance assessor rang to say he was coming in on Friday, and hoped we could meet him at the property; we gave him instructions and a meeting time. It was heartening that they were so on the ball, though we had no idea how to deal with such calculations. It was all moving fast.

By Friday morning, word of a community meeting was circulating again. When we reached the township, there were vehicles parked in every available space: police, fire, government and what looked like a few army trucks—high-level brass, for sure. Looming particularly large, though, was a petrol tanker parked near the bakery, with lines of plastic jerrycans beside it. There was more uniformed brass than you see on Anzac Day. 'I guess the world knows where Kinglake is now,' said Sean wryly.

It was cold and people were lining up for hot food. We once again gathered near the shire offices for the news update: the police expressed particular concern about the increasing number of signs threatening to shoot looters, and announced they would heavily staff the police station twenty-four hours a day, seven days a week, for as long as necessary and would respond quickly to calls. There was so much raw emotion about that the police couldn't assume that residents wouldn't act on their threats. Sean had remarked on the way down that there were definitely people who didn't belong here getting in on the back roads.

The army was on its way too; now I really felt my taxes were at work. Police personnel were already stretched and we needed a high level of community supervision, not to mention vital ongoing measures like the clearing of roads and damping down of fire hotspots. Generators were being brought in for surviving properties, as it would be some time yet before power was restored; that petrol tanker was three-quarters filling car tanks, or handing out a jerrycan. A rumour spread through the crowd like wildfire that the tanker had been sent by one of the transport unions and the driver had fronted the roadblock and told police he wasn't stopping until he got fuel to the people on the mountain. I have no idea whether it was true or not, but that big guy dishing out petrol became our hero that day. He didn't stop the hose until the truck was empty, and he vowed that another one would take its place the next day.

The word also went around that the owner of the local IGA supermarket was opening his doors so that people could get essential supplies. He too had been without power for a week, so all the perishable goods had gone, his business melted away on the floor. We lined up and took a number written on a scrap of paper. The supermarket staff took us around in the dark with a torch, to get candles, toilet paper or anything else we wanted; there was no charge, except a token amount for cigarettes and alcohol. Once the shelves were empty, that was it. The supermarket owner also went down in the book of great community-minded people that day. God knew when those shelves would be restocked.

There was a pile of daily newspapers on the footpath, which people could also take free of charge. Many pages were devoted to the fires, which were already being declared Australia's biggest natural disaster. Names of the dead were emerging: some we knew, some we didn't. One we did know was the bright young woman who worked at the supermarket. Another smiling face hit us like a brick—it was Alan O'Gorman, the nice agent who had sold us Number 59 and was always up for a chat when we ran into him. He'd died, with his wife and son, at Humevale, leaving behind a twin son and daughter.

The café was receiving goods by the truckload: food supplies, tools, more clothes, plastic goods, extension leads and the like, but no shoes. Maddie Duthie was still working like a Trojan to help sort it all out. Sean had picked up asbestos suits and a large sieve. We'd been warned about the dangers of asbestos in burnt-out properties and Sean has worked around enough building sites over the years to know what lurks in them, but he was hell-bent on checking out the rubble at Number 59 to see what might have survived. As we headed for the car, a convoy of power-company trucks came into the main street—dozens of them, crawling slowly through, parting the traffic and heading for the main sub-station and the pylons. We felt like dancing in the street. Things were on the move.

We met the insurance assessor later that morning. He was shaking his head and kept expressing his shock at what he'd witnessed on the drive up the mountain, though he'd been in the business for many years. He'd seen images on TV, but coming in so soon after the event was a sobering experience, even for an insurance veteran. For us, the meeting turned out to be little more than a formality. Two properties completely written off, the garden gone—no argument, just sign on the dotted line. He also offered some good advice on how to deal with it all, the likely time scale for payouts, and what should happen with the destroyed cars.

Then, out from under the rubble of the front shed emerged a little creature. It was Bonnie, the Smiths' dark grey cat. She made a beeline for the assessor, rubbing around his legs and letting rip with the meows. Sean and I were overjoyed, and indulged her with pats and cuddles. It reduced the insurance man to a heap. 'Is this your cat? Has it been missing all this time?' he asked, clearly battling a lump in his throat. The Smiths had sighted her over the past week, but then she'd disappeared. An outdoor farm cat, she was used to being self-sufficient and we'd promised to keep an eye out for her. She'd always been a regular visitor at Number 59 and her appearance made our day—another survivor.

Sean suited up for his sifting efforts. I was as concerned about sharp tin, shattered glass and jagged nails as I was about asbestos and other particles that might still be hanging in the air. Then there was the chimney, still standing but cracked and precarious. Parts of the house site had already been disturbed, as an initial forensic crew had checked it out. These white-suited teams had become part of the landscape, as every property had to be looked at before it could be cleared for clean-up. The ever-cranking rumour mill suggested that fleeing people had left their cars in panic and run onto properties looking for shelter. The scale of the task was incomprehensible.

Sean was gone for hours and reappeared covered in charcoal, soot and dust. He was carrying a heavy plastic bag. 'I found a few things by working out where the rooms were,' he said. Out of the bag came a blackened ring with the distinctive shape of the one I'd made with my mother and grandmother's engagement-ring stones; the rubies and diamonds were encrusted with burnt matter. A delicate antique gold chain had also survived, but was now black. The rest of the jewellery had fused into a lump—it had completely melted and then re-solidified. A solid bronze Buddha head emerged next, unscathed. 'There's a bit of karma for you,' Sean said.

But the most surprising thing was a cheap, plaster statue of four Christmas choirboys, with the word 'Noel' written across them. My mother had owned it since she was a little girl; Noel was her name, because she was born on Christmas Day. Every year this figure—probably bought in one of the old-fashioned Woolworths stores found in small New Zealand country towns—took pride of place on the mantelpiece at Christmas-time. We examined it now: the choirboys' red hoods had been scorched off, but the 'Noel' was still visible—that this had survived when cast-iron cookware had melted was miraculous. We bundled it up and put it in a corner of John's shed. 'We'll get all this cleaned up. You never know, they might come up all right,' Sean said.

The next few days passed in a jumble of information (and emotional) overload. It was now the eve of the seventh day since hell had hit us head-on, yet this didn't really dawn on us—it seemed like it had happened yesterday.

We could only deal with issues as they arose. What we needed now were sturdy work clothes, overalls, replacement boots. Sean was managing to rip everything on ragged fence wire, roofing iron, and glass—and he was still wearing his melted Blundstones. We decided on another trip to Whittlesea on Saturday morning.

Brad called to say they were just getting their flights home. He was distressed and very restless: they hadn't been able to settle in Melbourne—everything around them seemed irrelevant. In the rush to get them to safety, I'd overlooked their trauma and pain.

They'd lived through that hellish event too, and then been left to their own devices; they didn't have on-tap counsellors, they'd had to help each other through. I felt guilty and remiss that I hadn't connected them to some of the services available.

The second drive to Whittlesea was even starker. What we'd missed on the first trip came into sharp focus on the second. The crèche and pre-school, and one of the primary schools, were gone; the names of insurance companies had been sprayed on ruined cars as a mark of ownership. A line of vehicles were again trying to get through the roadblocks, but being turned back. It was a relief when that trip ended.

At the material-aid centre, we discovered that a truckload of heavy workwear and boots had arrived. A practical gift, and they'd even supplied staff to fit it properly. Kitted out with overalls, work gloves, safety glasses and gear that could take some punishment meant we could go back onto the property and avoid injuries. Sean was still pursuing his replacement driver's licence.

As we walked out of the centre, running towards us was Kane Smith from next door. The thirteen-year-old was up for a big hug, then he looked at Sean and the shoulders slumped. 'Sorry, I let your drum kit burn,' he said. Sean had lent him a practice kit when he showed an interest. 'No, you didn't, mate. There was nothing you could have done about that,' Sean replied. In racing to catch us, Kane had pulled himself away from something far more exciting to a sports-mad teenager—some Australian Rules footballers and members of the Australian cricket team had arrived at the relief area. For Kane the thought of meeting, let alone getting a few bowling tips from, Shane Warne was enough to wipe out traumatic recent memories for the moment; it was pure gold to see him so excited. You couldn't have put a price on the presence of those sporting stars, particularly for kids who had lost homes, schools, friends or a close relative.

I had no desire to look for more general clothing at this point. Our friend Gretha Edwards had called from Steels Creek to say she'd cleaned out her wardrobe and had a suitcase full of clothes for me. She and husband Tim had fought to an exhausted standstill to save their luxury bed-and-breakfast property, with guests sheltering inside, when the fire swept down the national park that forms their rear boundary. They'd lost all Tim's building-business equipment, their sheds, cars and tanks; they'd also lost neighbours. But Gretha had taken the time to put together enough clothes for a core work wardrobe. 'We're about the same height and colouring,' she offered in a matter-of-fact way. She was right: everything fitted like a glove and gave me the confidence to step back out into the world without having to make any purchasing decisions or sort through donated goods.

On the Sunday, we made the decision to stay with Tania for a few days. The logistics of getting to work in a borrowed car appeared easier from somewhere closer. It was also an opportunity to try to regroup, to give Carissa some support and to examine our options. John and Julie also needed some thinking space, and rest. I was adamant about going back to work the next day, despite a raft of advice to the contrary. Many people felt it would prove too big an assault on my psyche while so many other decisions were required. As far as I was concerned, though, it would somehow be less stressful if I could feel I had things under control on that front, and it represented a return to something normal and routine. A bit like falling off the proverbial horse: the longer you wait to climb back in the saddle, the harder it becomes to do so.

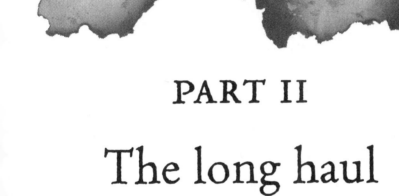

PART II

The long haul

6

A temporary dwelling

Just over a week after the fires, it seemed as if our feet hadn't touched the ground. Here we were, middle-aged, homeless, owning only what we stood up in, driving a borrowed car, and with a small menagerie to take care of.

Survivors of Black Saturday had limited accommodation choices in the short term: stay with family or friends, find something to rent in an already tight housing market, try an army tent in the initial emergency 'refugee' camp, stay in a motel, or borrow a caravan. The temporary accommodation provided by government and welfare authorities did not eventuate until months later, when they'd had time to assess the needs of the occupants of the 2200 homes that had been destroyed across the state.

John and Julie did not waver in their insistence that we stay with them for however long it took, declaring that this was the most logical solution. But our early decision to stay with Tania, at least as a first move, seemed more practical. However, by day three in Eltham not only were the sounds of the suburbs driving us crazy—the crashing rubbish truck, kids on their way to school, all-night traffic, slamming gates—but we felt as if some part of us had been amputated. Being away from our known, albeit dramatically altered, environment was a stressful wrench. We were also anxious about John and Julie being the only remaining residents at the lower end of Deviation Road, isolated and vulnerable. Sean and I agreed that we needed to be near Number 59 too, for the sake of the horses and to keep the property safe from marauders. So, by 21 February, two weeks after Black Saturday, we'd asked John and Julie if we could take up their offer and return to the mountain.

So, that weekend we ignored the skeptics and doomsayers, and four strong-minded, independent, self-sufficient and opinionated adults prepared to share a house. There were plenty of critics offering sage advice: we'd drive each other crazy; these sorts of arrangements never work; there'd be two women in one kitchen and two men with opposing views on how to do things; we'd have no personal space; John and Julie would want to sleep in, as they'd retired, whereas Sean and I would be up crashing about early in order to go to work. And what if the O'Connors were still there in a year's time and wouldn't budge? We heard it all, one way or another.

Amongst other things, though, the way John and Julie's house is configured meant we had a bedroom and dedicated bathroom in one section, divided from their sleeping quarters by a family room and kitchen, and we could use separate exits if necessary. One saving grace was that at this stage the moving process was easy: two carry bags did the job! When we arrived back at Number 48, a wardrobe and bedroom storage had already been cleared out to accommodate our needs. And John had not only organised space for our personal items but also set aside a corner of a shed for goods we would inevitably acquire along the way.

That corner became what will remain a lifelong joke between us. Sean decided to remain off work for several weeks in order to deal with a raft of practical issues, such as tending to goats and horses, organising replacement cars, putting together some basic items we'd need and keeping up surveillance on Number 59. In sifting the rubble one day, he'd come across the remains of his .22 rifle. Although the gun was housed in the mandatory lockable steel cabinet, the barrel had, he told us, 'bent like a banana' in the fire. Whether bullets had been set off by the heat, we dreaded to think. 'It could have been like the gunfight at the O.K. Corral over there,' he mused.

'I'll ring the police tomorrow and ask them what the procedure is for guns,' John offered. He and Julie had quickly started chasing up a variety of issues for us, to leave us free to concentrate on work, whereas they had time available during business hours. John later told us that he'd asked about the gun, but didn't want to reveal its whereabouts for fear of creating an unnecessary hassle. 'When they asked for a name, all I could think of was O'Brien. Well, it's Irish!' he said. From then on, our goods and chattels were stashed in 'the O'Brien corner'.

The first major item for diplomatic negotiation was the fact that we had the two dogs, Meg and Jazz, and John and Julie had Bertie the black cat. (Harley was staying on with Tania for further vet treatment and until we had our own place for him to come back to.) Meg and Jazz were used to being inside, but they'd never been exposed to cats, except the Smiths' bossy Bonnie, who could bluff them both. Give them a cornered Bertie, though, and we had the potential for a major incident. While it may seem odd for us to have felt the need to devise a coexistence strategy for the animals in the midst of more pressing concerns, the reality is that even close friends have fallen out over lesser matters. We determined to solve these sorts of issues, or at least attempt to, before they caused domestic strife. Given that Bertie was prone to doing what cats do best—sleeping for most of the day—it was agreed that the dogs would have the run of the enclosed house and garden area during daylight hours and then, once they'd been fed, they'd be confined to the large laundry while Bertie had a nocturnal ramble. For the most part, there was animal peace.

The relationship evolved day by day; there was no big official pow-wow about the rules of the house. John made it clear from day

The extraordinary snowfall in 2008 made Kinglake look like another world.

turday, 7 February 2009. By early afternoon, thick smoke clouds were roiling up the untainside.

All of a sudden, the fire started shooting over the ridge in our back paddock and we knew we were in for a fight.

Carissa was taking photos over her shoulder as we ran for safety.

day dawned on a radically changed and destroyed landscape.

One of the Wattle Glen firefighters kindly gave Harley some relief from his burnt paws.

A giant ash tree, which had graced the front verge, was reduced to dust.

It was a grim journey home.

e knew we'd lost the house, but were still heartbroken to see the smoking ruins of what had been
r happy home.

an bravely started trying to retrieve anything that had survived, but there wasn't much left.

As we headed towards town, we could see the wholesale destruction left by the fire.

...fter months of waiting for our land to be cleared and working out what to do next, we finally ...oved forward, building a barn on the site of the old house. It was basically like camping under a ...of, but we were pleased to be on our own patch again.

...by bit, our barn is becoming a home (albeit a temporary one).

At last, the 'Barn Mahal' is becoming a reality.

one that he wouldn't discuss money in any formal way either: it was, as far as he was concerned, the last thing to get stressed about. (Mind you, John is the sort of person who turns hostile if you try to buy him a cup of coffee while out and about.) Instead, we agreed we'd share food shopping and play the rest by ear as we went along. Sean and I were confident we'd find ways to share the load.

There was an unspoken assumption, mainly on our part, that we'd be there for a few months at most—after all, we'd be getting on with things pretty quickly now. But what we'd come to know and love over years of interaction as 'John being Greek' now manifested itself in adamant statements such as: 'These things always take much longer than we expect, so just get used to it and relax' and 'Never offer to do something for somebody unless you are prepared to do it no matter how long it takes. Even if you don't like that person, once the offer is made it must be fulfilled'. These opinions were peppered with some philosophical musings about the possible role of Nemesis and other ancient Greek deities in the outcome. The bottom line was that he meant it—we were in his charge, under his care, and there was no other consideration.

Right from the start, the two-women-in-a-kitchen thing simply wasn't an issue. None of us is fussy when it comes to food and, besides, both John and Sean are perfectly capable at the stove. Sean became the chief barbecuer, Julie and I would share whatever cooking indoors was needed, and John was the pasta king. Our mealtimes were sociable, full of laughter and conversation, and afterwards we rarely felt the need for television or any other entertainment. John, though, is a self-confessed television addict and has different sleeping patterns to the rest of the world, so Julie would record programs for him and he'd happily watch reruns of *Zulu* or whatever else took his fancy at 3 a.m.

The conversations we shared endlessly became a valuable tool for moving forward. To twist a cliché, four heads were better than two when it came to sifting through options, making plans or simply trying to fathom what we'd all been through. It even eased the process of Sean and I arranging temporary accommodation at Number 59 while we built a new house, something we decided on within a few weeks of the fires. We didn't want to be rushed into rebuilding, and the decision to first put up a barn came effortlessly. We'd been contemplating this in recent times anyway, as a value-adding replacement for the old sheds, and part of it could easily be fitted out for living in.

John is one of those people who shops around, and he'd already done the homework when it came to sheds and barns. There wasn't much he didn't know about sheds of every shape and size, and he still had the contacts from his own construction efforts, which meant that getting quotes and briefing the builders happened quickly.

'We could have an Amish barn-raising,' John joked. Sean and I had spent some time in Amish country in Pennsylvania and were amazed by how these technology-shy communities could erect a massive barn in two days with sheer people-power and not a modern tool in sight. Ours would be more reliant on a rigging crew and scaffolding. But 'Project Barn' became a focus for all of us—a light at the end of the tunnel, a plan for the future, no matter how basic at this stage.

As the weeks went by, one of the greatest challenges was to remain alert to psychological and physical events that might make or break how we reshaped our futures. There was no daily diagnosis of where our heads were at: instead, the newly constituted household adopted a 'We're all right' attitude and soldiered on. But when least expected, routine and mundane tasks turned into mental mountains that threatened to sideswipe us without warning. And John and Julie were living with our loss and pain as well as trying to analyse their own monumental experience.

One habit we continued was to make sure that all four of us were never away from the property at the same time: fears of being burgled, or invaded in some way, remained too strong. We were becoming insular, working in unison and not looking to anyone outside for help. We endlessly raked over the events of 7 February—how in the space of a few hours we'd gone from lightheartedly planning dinner to living through unbelievable destruction—comparing times, the warning signs, sights, sounds, smells, thoughts and feelings. It was as though we were making sure it wasn't all a dream, that the complete story was downloaded.

As we went through the motions of doing whatever it took to keep everything on some sort of even keel, it came as something of a surprise to realise we'd been with John and Julie for several weeks already. We'd discussed in great detail the options for getting our property cleaned up and the likely timelines we faced before we could reasonably expect to start even the temporary rebuilding process. Trying to think beyond that was impossible.

'Just relax,' John would say, in his philosophical way. 'Think of a figure and double it and, in the meantime, just relax. We'll work through it.' It was to become something of a household maxim.

7

Rebuilding a life

About a month after the fires, Sean and I hauled two wheel-barrows across the road to Number 59 to salvage what we could. There was nothing of any material value, but it was all that remained of our goods and chattels. The cars had been removed by insurers, only the melted Land Rover remaining—it was too dangerous to get at under the collapsed shed roof.

Sifting through the rubble was soul destroying, more an exercise in letting go than an attempt to find precious things. But retrieving some outdoor items filled a sentimental need. A cracked terracotta birdbath, which had provided us with hours of feathered fun watching from the deck, went into the wheel-barrow first. Remnants of a Columbian windchime off the side verandah joined it; the lovely little terracotta pots, strung together, had always appealed to me. There was also a bird feeder, a small plastic greenhouse, two horse-feeding troughs and a smiling plaster Buddha that had kept watch over the backyard for years. A French oak wine barrel had survived the flames, but it stayed in the backyard because it was too heavy for the two of us to carry.

We pulled our stash back to John and Julie's and stored it in 'the O'Brien corner' of their shed. Around this time the state government announced it was funding the clean-up of destroyed properties and we registered early for that process. Initially we had assumed that this work would have to come out of insurance payouts, and we had two properties in need. Insurance assessors warned that the clean-up bill could be as high as $20 000 if asbestos was found on a property, the chances of which were extremely high in older sheds and dwellings. For the uninsured, such a cost could have extinguished their chances of starting again.

At this point we had no clear idea of the next steps in a rebuilding process—just the clean-up seemed utterly daunting, not least the fallen and burnt trees littering every property. The local shire had already issued 'Dangerous Property' orders where chimneys were still standing and had given owners seven days to clean them up, which was more about highlighting legal liability than a realistic expectation of the work being achieved before the government-sponsored clean-up. But receiving such notices felt to us like an unreasonable, additional assault.

While our decision to stay and rebuild was made early on, it was a distant proposition. The period between dealing with the initial loss and reaching a point where you are capable of deciding how to replace the roof over your head is one of the toughest phases of the recovery process. And even once the decision is made, it isn't just a case of collecting the insurance money, planning your dream house and whistling up the builder, then throwing the house-warming party a few months later. Every step of the journey is littered with major emotional hurdles, traps for the unwary, rushed and perhaps regretted decisions, bureaucratic procedures, and more than a sprinkling of gratuitous advice. It confronts you with the very best of human nature and generosity, but also the very worst—opportunists and shysters who will steal, do a shoddy job or try the hard-sell.

We'd never before built a house from scratch and it was a very steep learning curve as we negotiated potentially costly pitfalls. When you add to the mix the emotional roller-coaster we were already on, which clouded sensible decision-making processes and would side-track us unexpectedly, it's no wonder that we felt we'd been smacked in the face when the enormity of the project inevitably hit. Building a house under normal conditions is a time-consuming process, from the planning to the supervision stages. We were also facing the prospect of re-establishing a garden from scratch—in itself a daunting proposition. We wondered if we had the energy to take it all on, or if it would be easier to simply buy something already established. And what was the best course in economic terms? That was the million-dollar question (so to speak!). What could we actually afford? Restoring value in a destroyed property is one thing; over-capitalising and becoming saddled with debt is quite another. We were very aware of the broader situation too—the nation was in the grip of a worldwide economic downturn, with no guarantees of ongoing employment or sympathetic banks awash with credit.

Once we decided what we could afford, then came the next raft of decisions. Where will we site the house? Should we build over the existing site, which already had plumbing and power, or build on another part of the property, which would mean having to construct even those basic services? It was overwhelming. Trying to envisage the entire project from beginning to end, in one go, was mentally paralysing. We realised we had to break it down into logical steps, and even then accept that our plans would need to be adaptable.

Our first step was having to come to terms with the physical destruction wrought by the fires. There is no prescriptive time-scale for this journey and each individual deals with it differently. For both Sean and me, gathering up anything salvageable was part of the weaning process. Strangely, each visit to Number 59 caused a graphic replaying in my head of what was lying under the rubble— my brain was archiving the colours, shapes and exact locations of contents. I felt no overwhelming grief for the loss of material things: compared to lives spared and lives lost, they were of little impor-tance. Rather, my visual itemising, often room by room, cupboard by cupboard and drawer by drawer, was involuntary. Sean, for his part, felt driven to try to find precious items that might have been spared; it was his way of still fighting the destructive monster.

Then, when sleep was elusive or while I was stuck in peak-hour traffic on the way to or from work, my brain would suddenly regurgitate the contents of the house. Quite ridiculous things: the bills stuck under a magnet on the fridge door and whether I'd thought to pay them; what was in the pantry, fridge and freezer; the china stored in boxes in the shed, which hadn't seen the light of day for years; the green suede shoes I'd bought in New York. I remember those shoes. They'd jumped out at me in a shop on Fifth Avenue: they were different to anything on offer back home and always drew lots of compliments. They were funky but flat and comfortable—a perfect case of fashion meeting functionality—and I still miss them. This constant rehearsal of our house contents had an unforeseen, helpful result, eventually leading to several logical lists. One was of goods and chattels that we had used constantly, another of things that rarely made an appearance. Sentimental items, family heirlooms, photographs and works of art fell into their own category.

Accepting that no amount of contents insurance could replace the irreplaceable was the second step in the recovery process. Your mother's jewellery, or a granddaughter's primary-school paintings, can never be replicated. Our books, amassed over years, Sean's extensive CD and vinyl record collections, his precious piano and drum kit—gone forever. We also found ourselves acknowledging that a fair proportion of our general household goods had been surplus to requirements—it is staggering how much 'stuff' we human beings can amass. 'Look at it as the ultimate decluttering exercise!'

one friend offered. And she was right. Who needed six salad bowls, horrible mugs that we'd replaced ages ago, or hoarded worn-out linen items that never saw the light of day? Their ghosts could be, and were, jettisoned painlessly, wiped off the list of things to occupy the brain. Bit by bit, it became a cathartic mental dumping exercise, a way of accepting what had gone and either giving it a decent, rueful send-off or putting it in the 'Good riddance!' basket.

It was important to deal with our finances in the same way. Trying to handle money issues when the brain still isn't functioning normally is a big ask. In this we were lucky to get wonderful counsel from people who went out of their way to share their own post-disaster experiences—how they had, for example, felt the need to spend money replacing things before they'd determined what they truly needed. One letter I received from an elderly woman urged me not to make the same mistake she had, racing out and buying everything new. While it felt good at the time, she said, a few years later she was faced with the expense of having to replace it all again at the same time. Staggering the buying process made sense. Others urged us to make do with as little as possible until the mental fog started to lift and our housing options become a lot clearer. We'd already determined to furnish any temporary accommodation with the donated goods we had stored, but the advice was encouraging and reinforcing.

Next we had to come to terms with the clean-up, which was scheduled for April. Many survivors found themselves clinging to their personal dust and rubble—macabre perhaps, but it was like honouring the dead. Whenever there was evidence that our ruins had been rifled by strangers, which happened on several occasions, we felt physically ill and uncontrollably angry. Once Sean came across some metal storage boxes which, having fused shut in the heat of the fires, had been jemmied open while we weren't around. He also found the charred contents of our shed scattered in all directions, and sheets of roofing iron dragged off to the side (clearly this had not been done by forensics people, who did you the courtesy of leaving an indicator when they visited). There were the children, aged only around ten, who John had chased off the site, only to cop a string of foul abuse. After the roadblocks were lifted, late in March, we saw people with metal detectors going over properties, looking for 'souvenirs'—our destroyed lives had become somebody else's entrepreneurial opportunity. 'I'm tempted to put up one of those "Keep off or you'll be shot" signs,' Sean said. It was sorely testing my non-violent principles as well.

For us, getting rid of the remains became a priority, but these things always take longer than you'd like. For us, as long as the debris was still there the phoenix couldn't rise from the ashes; we needed a blank canvas. The managers of the clean-up process had set up site offices in the township and the demolition convoys had become an integral part of the local traffic scene. Loaded to the hilt, large-muscle trucks, bulldozers and tracked vehicles with huge grabbing mechanisms would roar up the main-road hill to the designated landfill site, then come screaming back an hour later. 'We've been teaching the crews to get in touch with their feminine side,' one supervisor offered lightheartedly. The hard-heads of the industry were not used to being delicate about whether a daisy got squashed.

The managers were patient and understanding with our constant queries about timelines. There had already been occasions when the demolition crew had arrived at a property only to have the owners call a halt because they couldn't after all deal with seeing their material life dumped on the back of a truck. While we awaited our turn, Sean and I would try to sketch plans for a new home. Mostly, though, my paper either stayed blank or threw up a replica of our destroyed house. The old layout would tumble out automatically and stare back at me from the paper—it was frustrating, and doing nothing for my state of mind.

Then, at last, I reached a turning point. In one of our offloading sessions with John and Julie, I started to relate the things about Number 59 that we hadn't liked, found impractical or would have preferred to change. For example, the bathroom opening off the family room had always been a bugbear; so too was the small, impractical laundry, and the lack of built-in storage. This in itself was mentally confronting. How picky, obscene even, to be criticising what we would have had back in a heartbeat, warts and all, given the chance. But it worked. The more I conjured up the things I would have changed, the easier it became to turn to something new, and bit by bit an entirely different layout started to emerge.

Both Sean and I would play at refining it. We had no conflict over the basic concept, wanting it all to be as environmentally sustainable as possible, with no wasted spaces, everything having a practical purpose but also replicating the warmth and earthiness we'd injected into 'the Battlestar'. There was no thought of costing our ideas at this stage—rather, it was a cathartic focus on the future, a goal that could be aimed for one step at a time.

Now our attention turned to constructing the barn. Here it was a bonus to have a handy husband with an engineering brain who could manage the project. 'It will be really funky. Like a New York warehouse apartment,' Sean declared. (Well yes, bar the Manhattan skyline.) Thus was conceived what became known as 'the Barn Mahal'. It had to be American style, with a pitched roof and a mezzanine, and there was also instant consensus that it had to be red. Why, I don't know, except that barn and red seemed to go together.

'We'll put it where the house was. That way we can use the old septic tank and the paths and brick paving,' Sean said. 'Let's salvage and re-use what we can.' He went through reams of paper drawing up a big red barn, with his own engineering specifications. It would give us enormous leeway: comfortable enough to live in so we could spread the house-building process (and its financing), and providing adequate storage for cars and building equipment. And it would look amazing from the outside, rather than turning into one of those 'temporary' sheds that never quite gets removed or improved further down the track.

Clearing the site now became even more urgent. The goods being offered by friends and relief agencies had become a major issue, with good basic items having to be rejected or delayed for the simple reason that John and Julie's spare bedroom and sheds were already filling up and there was nowhere to store them. It hadn't taken long to go from owning only what we stood up in to having to buy extra coathangers and a shoe rack. Bigger items needed a different solution, and by April we'd hired a commercial storage unit off the mountain. There was a suggestion that shipping containers were being brought into the community as temporary storage, but for most residents this initiative seemed to fall through the cracks, so rather than relying on others we sourced and bought our own.

There were also rumours that philanthropic individuals were offering to provide a large storage facility for the community to share. Unfortunately, this initiative appeared to get bogged down in council arguments about where it should be situated, despite the fact that it could be used for community purposes later. We couldn't wait for the issue to be resolved so made our own arrangements. It proved to be an inspired decision, putting something substantial back on the property, providing the reassurance of lockable and secure storage, and rapidly paying for itself in saving us the costs of a commercial facility. Besides, we couldn't have bought a small garden shed for what this steel number cost us.

Money was a constant consideration. Our initial insurance payouts had been rapid, and our first use for this money was to clear all our debts. There were no 'handouts' in relation to Number 1 and nor should there have been; it is an investment and any investment carries a risk. But the financial reality was that it had gone from a renovated, rented asset to an unimproved block of land—the only remaining structure was the Hills hoist and even that was totally bent out of shape. We had no hope of rebuilding there, even if we could raise the energy to do so, but at least we could sell part of it if our finances became stretched. The remaining insurance payouts we earmarked for building our new house, though the finishing and furnishing of that will occur over a longer period of time.

But many other people, once they had paid out their mortgage—a requirement by banks in many cases where properties were totally destroyed in the fires—still owed some of the original amount and only had inadequate contents insurance to subsidise rebuilding or buying elsewhere. It has frequently been questioned why people weren't adequately insured, with much tut-tutting about the stupidity of this. But nothing is as simple as it seems on the surface. Most tenants, for instance, never think to insure their belongings with contents insurance—indeed, nor did I when I rented properties in the past.

Following the fires it became rapidly clear to us that, where insurance is concerned, you get what you are prepared to pay for. I've yet to meet anybody from the fire-affected areas who says insurance will go close to covering their losses, even when they had better-than-average cover. The reality is that it is almost impossible to accurately calculate what a property and its contents are truly worth. Even a room-by-room calculation will generally be an underestimate. Usually, we think in terms of the larger items— lounge suites, television sets, bedroom furniture, fridge, washing machine, dishwasher, etc.—the 'big ticket' items that we don't replace very often. But what can seriously trip up the maths are the sums for replacing daily basics: the contents of a linen cupboard that services a family of four or five (not including the doona cover you bought on a whim, or the spare stuff for unexpected guests), or every item in kitchen drawers and cupboards such as day-to-day cutlery, implements, crockery, glassware, cookware and electrical appliances. Now apply this equation to every room, and outside too. In our case, in addition to all the structures and infrastructure, we had also lost the cars and the shed and garage contents.

In a community such as Kinglake, reliance on motor vehicles is extremely high. Public transport was non-existent when we arrived here and only now, post-disaster, is there anything remotely resembling a regular bus service. The loss of motor vehicles on Black Saturday was huge, even on properties where houses survived, and replacing them was an early and urgent need, particularly for families with children. Car manufacturers offered new-model 'bushfire relief vehicles' for between six and twelve months to people who had not been insured. Such vehicles gave people breathing space while they sorted out their finances, but the recipients still faced having to buy something else in a few months' time. Of course, the loan vehicles were great grist for the rumour mill: Hah! There they are living in a caravan and driving a brand-new car. Or: They didn't lose their house, but they've got a swank new set of wheels. In our case, we replaced our three comprehensively insured cars with a 'workhorse' dual-cab ute that would hold its value, and a secondhand, economical runabout.

It was mid-April before we received the call to let us know it was our turn for demolition and clean-up. We were required to be present, to sign the authorisation and ensure the crew knew what was going and what was staying. As the date got closer, feelings of massive emotional upheaval were fighting with the desire to have the job done so we could grit our teeth and just get on with things.

Clean-up day dawned in typical Kinglake fashion—it was freezing and the wind was howling, bringing intermittent bursts of sleet. Sean realised that he hadn't yet taken down the expensive fittings that had survived on the otherwise melted bore header tank (a bit of plumbing recycling). But it was all still sitting up on the high stand, and Sean had recently injured his wrist badly while lifting heavy debris.

'I'll go up the ladder and get them,' I offered.

He laughed. 'You, the vertigo queen, up a ladder with a bloody big wrench!' True: heights and I are a bad combination. But John has the same problem, so I was determined to do it. The three of us beat our way through the weather before the trucks turned up just after dawn. 'I'll be okay as long as the two of you are holding the ladder steady,' I assured everyone (including myself). Up I went, rung by rung, clutching a seriously oversized wrench. Halfway up, that swaying, sick, dizzy feeling kicked in. I had to use both hands to get the wrench around the fittings. Terrific! But somehow it all happened, though by the time I was back on the ground every muscle from feet to backside was screaming and shaking and my head was spinning. It felt good to have faced my fear, though the phobia remains.

We headed into our shipping container for some shelter while we waited for the crew to turn up. We reminisced about the entire suburbs of containers converted into simple dwellings which we'd passed while driving across America some years earlier, and the ones turned into dockside workshops in parts of Asia, and wondered why greater use wasn't made of them elsewhere. As a recyclable item, we decided it was a winner—certainly better than being left to bob hazardously about in oceans. A coat of paint and a bit of landscaping, and that container is staying.

The sounds of heavy machinery announced the arrival of the demolition crew. They stood on the front lawn shivering, in spite of their polarfleece jackets. 'Welcome to Kinglake, guys, and this isn't even winter,' I said. They hopped from foot to foot and I realised that their sensitivity-towards-fire-victims training was kicking in: not wanting to rush us, politely engaging in conversation when they'd rather be in a warm cabin. Sean walked them through what we wanted retained. It wasn't much—the greasetrap and bore entrance in addition to the paving and the septic tank. They donned asbestos suits, set up a toxic-materials monitor and fired up the machinery. It hit me harder than I had expected when I saw the first scoopful of debris being unceremoniously flung into the truck. It was easier to walk away and leave them to it, without looking back.

By the end of the day, Number 59 was a blank space. There was a levelled area where the house had stood; the once-flourishing front garden was a sea of track-marks; the driveway and side lawn were sporting deep, muddy grooves. We were going to need a clean-up after the clean-up. But the razed landscape made it easier for us to envisage the future, and from that day the barn project became our primary focus. It was a nightly subject of discussion with John and Julie. For John it became something positive to help plan and pore over, though he was careful never to offer gratuitous advice. The weather was continuing to be unkind—wet, muddy and windy. We were also at the mercy of the council permit process, which was proving to be slow and tedious; it took weeks even to receive the engineering drawings for the structure. Meanwhile, life went on: we went to work, came home to John and Julie's, and continued planning the fit-out. There were moments when our objective seemed to retreat further into the distance and our guilt grew about our extended imposition on John and Julie. They, on the other hand, were never anything other than encouraging. They'd been through the experience of building from scratch and well understood the delays and frustrations. We all took things day by day.

John and Julie also appreciated our decision to opt for 'camping' in the barn once it was built, rather than rushing to build a house. For us, the connection to our land was very strong, and we wanted to be close to the project, not travelling from a distance every weekend to try to get things done. At the same time, the prospect of having to trawl the private rental market, to maintain another property and have limited leisure time to get on with rebuilding our lives, was a total turn-off.

The barn was designed and ordered by May, but then we had to grind through the bureaucratic processes. While it is recognised that displaced people need to get back into accommodation as quickly as possible, there is an underlying concern that some might find their converted sheds and barns eminently liveable and affordable, and not move on to building new homes; temporary dwellings are not good for rate revenue, or for property values and community 'amenity'. In our case, the delays appeared to be more a matter of misplaced paperwork and a local government struggling to cope with the enormity of the task. We just wanted our own roof over our heads.

'Just build your barn and move into it. If anybody gives you a hard time about any of it then tell them personally from me to go and get rooted!' It wasn't the sort of conversation I would have expected to be having with the head of a government body, but Christine Nixon, chair of the state's Bushfire Reconstruction Authority, was accessible, touchable, and oozed warmth and empathy. 'I'm interested in getting people housed and back on their properties, not in bloody councils holding up bloody permits,' she said. Her support and practical, no-nonsense approach almost reduced me to tears. It was in the middle of a rebuilding expo, where she was happy to be personally approached, and it made the difference between us punching on or giving in and putting up a 'For Sale' sign rather than battle endless delays.

While the barn would put some initial value onto our devalued land, we were conscious that common sense had to prevail. It needed to meet our need for a temporary dwelling and have a future use, but not become an overcapitalised white elephant once a house went up. We started to sensibly plan a small kitchen, living area, bedroom and bathroom. I had only one demand: even if it was a barn, I wanted a bathtub—soaking in a bath is my stress-reliever and escape hatch. We calculated that it would take two years to fully execute the sort of house we wanted, so there had to be some domestic pleasures in the meantime.

Mind you, there were months of work ahead just to get the barn in liveable condition. Whatever time you think such a project will take, think again: concrete floors take longer than expected to dry, tradesmen need to attend for anything that requires compliance certificates. But once the building materials were delivered in late June and the construction crew swung into action, the basic structure was up in less than a week. The concrete slab was poured a week later and we were itching for it to dry so we could plot out an interior.

Staying with John and Julie during this time was invaluable—instead of having to drive from elsewhere, we could simply go across the road. We could also devote any spare time to searching for practical and cost-effective items. This is the point at which temporary accommodation can turn into a serious money-pit, and a mantra formed in our heads: 'This isn't a house. It is a temporary dwelling.' While it would provide additional living space in the future, it had to be able to be converted back into a straight barn without too much hassle if that's what some future owner wanted.

We installed water tanks first, to ensure we could harvest any rain and have a ready supply, albeit from a tap on the tank initially. Then we began looking for building materials that could be salvaged, and sourcing the best options for anything new. It was an indulgent husband and my longing for a bath that turned up an astonishing stroke of luck and transformed a big red shed into the Barn Mahal. Sean answered an advertisement for a spa bath with all the fittings, pump and accompanying shower for $200. 'I'll go and check it out. If it's in good condition, that's cheap therapy. We couldn't buy a bath and separate shower unit for that,' he pronounced.

A few hours later, I received an excited phone call. Not only was the spa unit in top condition, but the seller was demolishing an entire house and had offered anything else we could use. He wanted to get on with building his new home and didn't have the time to sell everything individually. We offered him, in addition to the $200 for the spa, $2500 for whatever we could dismantle. This included the kitchen and all its appliances, sinks, mixer taps and cabinetry, as well as bathroom vanity units, new toilet suites, ceiling fans, sunblock blinds, boxes of double power points, wardrobe fittings, even some carpet. We hooked up the trailer, thanked the Lions Clubs for the tools they'd given us that would do the job, and linked up with our friends Patsy and Jimmy Gansen, who'd driven up from Gippsland to help.

It took a weekend to dismantle and carefully stack our treasure trove in preparation for several trips from the opposite side of Melbourne and back up the mountain. By dusk on Sunday, the seller was curious about what we were going to do with it all. When we explained our situation, he wanted to give our money back. No way, Sean and I agreed; what we'd bought for a minuscule amount would make for an unexpectedly comfortable temporary home. It was the ultimate piece of recycling.

John's large shed came to the rescue for storing it all. The kitchen set-up was top of the range, twenty years old but in pristine working order. 'How insane is that? A designer kitchen in a barn,' I kept saying. It was a far cry from the couple of flat-pack cupboards, a single sink and a cooktop that had been on our initial plan. 'When people see it installed, they'll think we spent a big chunk of grant money on it,' I said. Paranoia dies hard.

Towards the end of August we had the shell of a dwelling. Patsy and Jimmy loaned us their caravan, which initially sat outside. At least there was shelter from the weather and a place to make a cup of tea while we were working there, and we could gradually move bits and pieces in so they'd be on hand when needed. Meanwhile we continued to develop the house plans, intending to mark out the exact house site before committing the design to draughting paper.

We had lost about 3.5 kilometres of fencing in the fires and wanted to replace it as soon as possible. Apart from anything else, we wanted our horses to come home, not only to have our 'tribe' back together but also because pasture was growing like crazy. That lush growth could provide vital feed for a neighbour's flock of sheep that had eaten his paddocks out. In a connected community it makes sense to share resources: we had grass (and lots of it!) but neither the time nor the energy to slash it, whereas our neighbour was having to bring in fodder to keep his livestock going. A bonus was that the sheep would happily eat the weeds that were thriving in the post-fire regrowth.

Our goats also needed a secure boundary. We'd had to bring them back from temporary accommodation off the mountain, after the perpetually curious male, Billy Bob Thornton (an escapologist at the best of times), took a special liking to the rose bushes poking through nearby fences and started leading the others out through the fence on raids. Back at Number 59, they'd generally stick on the property, bar the occasional excursion, but with no fences we couldn't replant anything or it would be instantly eaten.

Immediately after the fires, there just weren't enough fencing contractors available, even for those who could afford the full replacement cost. Within weeks, a voluntary fencing group called Blaze Aid was formed by Kilmore East farmers Kevin and Rhonda Butler. They had lost their fences on Black Saturday and in order to secure their 1500 sheep, rallied help from friends, family and volunteers to get the job done in a week. The Butlers were so grateful that they decided to keep the volunteer crews going. The deal was that if a property owner supplied the materials, they would send in a crew to get it all installed. After numerous knock-backs from professional fencing contractors, we put our name on the Blaze Aid list. The Blaze Aiders copped a lot of flak for supposedly doing fencing contractors out of paid work, but the latter weren't exactly lining up on our property (and in fact we still haven't had calls back from some of those we approached).

The service was amazing. When our turn came, a Blaze Aid team arrived first to assess the materials needed, ordered these at a better price than we'd been able to source, had the goods delivered instantly and turned up with the volunteer crew on the appointed days. Nothing is that simple, though, and before anything happened we had to have full site inspections done to locate any fibre-optic cables and so avoid a post-hole digger blacking out the town's internet and phone connections. It was July when they did start work, and the weather was absolutely foul. Many of the volunteers were camping overnight in tents and caravans, others driving hundreds of kilometres each day. They worked like crazy, snatching a coffee out in the rain or politely asking if they could move an old outdoor table behind the barn in order to cut the ice out of the wind for their smoko. They were soothing, kind and reassuring human beings who brought a lot of light our way. A few extra little jobs were done as well, the resourceful team leader Craig using his tractor to hoist our new header tank onto the stand—a task that would have required us putting together our own crew. In November the Butlers received Victoria's Local Heroes Award 2010; no one deserved it more.

The psychological boost afforded by our renewed feeling of ownership and security was immeasurable. I'd apologetically asked if the Blaze Aiders could start with the front fence, because that demarcation line seemed to me to say that people owned this property and were going to live here, that this was our space. 'I know it seems crazy when there's a main-road boundary that needs doing,' I said. One of them replied, 'That's not crazy, love. We had one person who wanted a gate to go up first. She wanted a gate back because it made her feel secure.' When I arrived home from work and saw the front fence back in place, I cried like a baby.

8

Lost
landscapes

I N September 2009, we sat and ate pies with good friends who
had come to tell us they were quitting the community for good,
even though they would retain property here. These were people
who had been involved in local issues, who cared what happened,
who stood up to be counted, people of high intelligence and great
humour, with whom we had shared many good times.

'It's a totally different place now. It just feels weird. It's not
what we came here for,' they told us. They'd sat in the Kinglake
pub carpark on 7 February and watched their just-renovated house
burn down across the road. They stayed near the mountain in
the aftermath, but found the loss of their familiar surroundings
gutting. Others in their circle had also made the decision to go,

so their familiar circle and their environment had fractured at the same time.

Even by November 2009, nine months after Black Saturday, whichever road you took to get onto or off the mountain you were faced with a long stretch of devastation before you entered an unburnt zone. Amidst all the rhetoric and spin associated with government and community rebuilding efforts, we heard plenty about community re-engagement, community healing and community renewal. Yet the significance of having to live with such a dramatically changed landscape seemed to me to be little acknowledged. Nobody quite put their descriptive finger on the fact that survivors were grieving for a lost collective environment—sights, sounds and smells—as well as for their own personal surroundings.

For some time we avoided familiar and much-loved drives, down to Strathewen or through Flowerdale. There was too much visual and human pain. Driving to and from work or elsewhere started to get a little easier as time went by. 'The Windies' acquired some sparkling new 'furniture' to replace the melted road markers and signs: freshly painted white lines, luminous audio strips to indicate the edges, 60 km/h speed limits (previously 80 km/h), and flashing, solar-powered warnings for motorcyclists to slow down.

The speed with which this and other roads were restored to driveable condition was phenomenal. But the landscape cannot be reinstated in such a way, and will not be the same again in my lifetime on the mountain. Precarious corners that lost underpinning soil and rock remain a little flaky and are signposted with warning markers; former blind bends are no longer blind; at night, the city skyline is now visible in spots where no lights or views penetrated before. The vegetation that clothed the landscape has pretty much gone and the contours of the stripped roadway against the side of the mountain can be clearly seen across the gullies.

My former 'Time to relax, you're nearly home' landmarks on this road, just after St Andrews, now evoke a sometimes crushing sadness. This is the fireline, the spot where the flames were snatched by the changing wind and sent hurtling up the mountain. That frontier is still clearly visible—on one side the land is green and untouched, on the other it is black and barren—and causes a jolt. There is no longer a big green umbrella to drive under near the apex: instead, raw stumps ooze sap and bulldozed road verges are bald and rutted. 'Closed' signs populate the entrances to bush-walking trails. Even a minor shower of rain turns the naked rock to waterfalls; a downpour engenders a veritable river of blackened mud sluicing down the culverts and over the road. The breezy, verdant drive, with its diverse landscape and wildlife, has turned into a toxic trip. Sometimes I zip through it as a matter of course, but at other times it hits me hard and there's a lump in my throat for the entire journey.

The higher up the mountain you go, the greater the destruction; the steeper the slope, the greater the momentum the fire gathered. The national park has become a forest of twisted black twigs, in places looming like a gigantic, bad hair transplant. Some trees have resprouted, but it is a deformed growth, a desperate survival mechanism. Not much of the undergrowth has returned, although tenacious mosses greened up some spots after continuous rain in September, and by spring 2009 there was a cascade of purple heath tumbling sporadically over the rock face.

The experts say that the moss will allow self-seeded eucalypts and wattles to get a foothold; other people believe the fire created such intense heat that it killed the seed in many places. Now, months later, there is generally nothing here for wildlife to eat and they are conspicuous by their absence. Road kill is disheartening at the best of times, but to see it in this charcoal landscape is tragic.

Even heading along Deviation Road could cause a stomach lurch. Every trip to any part of the mountain turned up something new, different or changed: the pine plantation at Pheasant Creek flattened and more roadside trees gone, temporary dwellings on neighbouring properties, buildings that seemed to have sprung up overnight and without thought, the hundreds of walnut trees in John's paddock now dead and showing no signs of regeneration— another everyday sight gone. Later in the year, drier spring conditions saw wood smoke hanging in the air for weeks as people burned off their combustible debris. It didn't matter whether or not you had suffered property loss, changes like these affected everybody.

At the same time, every familiar nook and cranny on our own place was irrevocably changed. No more the joy of seeing spring buds or autumn leaves blazing against the blue-grey native foliage; no more enjoying the endless pleasures provided by the huge trees with their diverse wildlife; no more flowering gums for the butterflies. Our extensive and much-admired garden had been our haven: a walk down the brick paths to pick roses and Easter daisies, admiring the towering rhododendrons and camellias, trees to sit under, and, of course, for the birds to enjoy. But re-landscaping had to take a back seat to getting a roof over our heads and by the end of 2009 we had not even reached the stage of practical planning for the levelled site.

Once, almost everything we planted was guaranteed to thrive under the nurturing canopy. Now plants would snap and fall over before they could get a proper foothold. A future garden will bear no resemblance to what was there before: any revegetation plans will have to take account of the absence of windbreaks and shade cover, as even a decent shower of rain pounds in with nothing to break the fall. There are still trees that may or may not survive; others have a tenuous grip on the earth and could succumb to an aberrant wind. Only time will tell.

The best-case scenario, we have been told, is that it will take seven years to establish a good, basic garden. The renewal of those fabulous old-growth trees that money couldn't buy will be for future generations to enjoy. In addition to any other considerations, good plants are not cheap and such purchases have to take their place on the list, behind more pressing needs. There is also the matter of what we, and many others in the same situation, should and shouldn't plant again, what might affect our bushfire risk levels. With such a changed environment, what will take hold will depend on the changed composition of the soil and the new levels of exposure to the elements. Where new trees are located matters hugely now: away from buildings to minimise the chances of ignition and of filling the gutters or house surrounds with leaves.

The views from every part of the property have also been totally altered. Now the panorama is of paddock and sky, the barn windows providing the only frame. The new housing estate near the township, previously not visible from Number 59 because of the tree coverage, is now a conspicuous suburb, complete with street lights. Parts of the main road, also once blocked from view by our careful planting, are wide open and we are on view to the passing traffic. The distant ranges that now form part of the vista were in the past blocked by bush. Some of this bestows beautiful new views, but other aspects have been an assault on the senses. The curtains that we'd drawn on our part of the world have been rudely pulled back—it's like having a shower with the blinds up, in full view of the neighbourhood.

Another associated but unanticipated transformation has been the change in the sounds around us. The stripping of so much vegetation has created a wind tunnel at Number 59, and the sheltered backyard where once barely a leaf stirred on a windy day is now prey to noisy, swirling and buffeting gusts. Every tyre passing on the main road is loud and obvious, and there seems to be traffic day and night. Previously, we were never conscious of such a volume; it was difficult to tell whether cars and trucks were on the distant main road or pounding down Deviation Road. Chainsaws, mulchers, power-tools, trucks and tractors have turned the mountain peace into a constant racket as people frantically work to clear blocks and restore their lives. At weekends, there's the constant rumble of tourist traffic; Sundays have ceased to be sleep-in occasions. It is likely to be thus for the foreseeable future.

That much-discussed local topic—the weather—has presented another challenge. The rain that deserted us the year before the fire has barely let up. From autumn 2009 it seemed heavier than usual, incessant, and loaded with hail. 'It's like it used to be when we first came here,' Sean remarked frequently, as winter tailed off into spring. When it was dry everywhere else, the mountain was subject to a torrent—either that or maddening, gale-force wind. Our new water tanks were constantly overflowing; outdoor activity would bog down for weeks. On the plus side, though, there was a sense of everything being washed clean, refreshing catchments, sending up dense new growth (weeds and all) from barren black earth. The rivulets came down the slopes like they used to, heading for rivers and streams.

The undue rains also caused the remnants of our herb and vegie garden to have insane growth spurts. Dill that once waved low, feathery foliage in the breeze hurtled to shrub proportions; the parsley grew to more than a metre high; the globe artichokes looked like small trees. Even with zealous watering, they had never behaved like that. The garden beds, which were bereft of foliage but which we weeded out with hopes of starting to replant, soon fostered a miniature forest of messmates, and baby wattles that sprouted like a carpet; sorrel invaded the paddocks. Whatever the fire had left behind in the soil changed its composition too. I had to have a new lemon tree; culinary life is incomplete without one. But whereas they'd previously grown without much attention, producing bumper crops, the new ones just looked sad and dropped their leaves once they were in. Bulbs we'd never seen flower before suddenly barrelled to the light.

While immediate physical changes were obvious, for us, like many other survivors, simply trying to regroup and keep our loved ones safe masked the horror of the physical destruction on all sides. By the time six months had passed, though, the environmental impacts were causing widespread grief. Some members of the community were threatening to chain themselves to trees in an effort to stop the wholesale removal of what remained of our precious flora; the contractors brought in to remove 'dangerous', remnant tall timbers became a much-abused species. (We stopped them in Deviation Road after they sliced through what seemed to be healthy and resprouting trees. On that occasion we were on the receiving end of the abuse as the crew, their work interrupted, packed up and left.) While many residents had little choice but to remove large dead trees if they were to rebuild safely, and the removal of anything in danger of toppling onto roads was obviously justifiable, the fact is that much of the initial destruction was carried out insensitively and without consultation. It was difficult enough for residents to inventory the plants that needed to be removed from our own properties, let alone to handle the seemingly random ripping that was taking place on public land. The middle section of Deviation Road looked like a logging coupe—a gouged, ragged, splintered mess.

And just to drive it home with a cruel irony, even our pastures began to fill up with weeds, the opportunistic noxious flora that we'd battled for so long to eliminate. And these weren't just any weeds, but the most tenacious; they populated the road verges as well. It would be a brave shire council that dished out weed-eradication notices to private landholders unless it has got its own roadside in order. The blackberries, too, were having a ball; thistles were back, and big; turnip weed scattered its loaded seed-heads to the four winds; cape weed was choking anything in its path. The surrounding state and national parks constitute a potential nightmare, as they too offer an open-slather opportunity for the invaders. Our task seemed overwhelming: there were months of work ahead just on the weed front.

For some people, the combination of personal trauma and such massive destruction of their surroundings, followed by extreme and ongoing environmental change, was too hard to come to terms with. It was the catalyst for many to leave the area forever, and there were stories of people who couldn't drive back into the community at all, the firelines a psychological barrier they just couldn't cross. Around 40 per cent of any community, it is estimated, will leave following a major disaster. Kinglake is reaching that point, and in the case of further-flung places such as Marysville, where local employment has been annihilated, the figure is expected to be much higher.

'This is not the place I came to live in. What it meant has gone' sits at one end of the response spectrum; 'Nature is amazing: it will regenerate. It's still a beautiful place to be' is at the other. Many people are still hovering somewhere in the middle. Those with little choice but to make the financial most of their land simply had to accept it, but of course that didn't mean they were unscarred by the experience. There have also been divided opinions among couples, one partner wanting to return while the other can't face the daunting workload or constant reminders of that fateful day. Others began rebuilding and then just walked away as it all proved too much.

And as you try to deal with your particular challenges, the people around you are also making life-altering decisions, dealing with personal demons, reordering priorities and just trying to move forward as best they can. It changes the way they are and how they interact, and in so doing irrevocably transforms entire communities. On the mountain, houses and land have been sold to new residents since the fires, many of whom had absorbed the views on weekend visits, then discovered that this part of the world was in commuting distance and more affordable than an inner location.

My Ash Wednesday mentor (a colleague who lost her house in the 1983 fires that razed parts of South Australia and south-western Victoria) identified this phenomenon in her community too, and says that twenty-six years later it is still divided into those who were there before the fires and those who moved in afterwards. The construction activity and ongoing clean-up is finite, of course, but we are destined to live with it for a long time yet. What will the overall neighbourhood be like in another year, two years, five years? Familiar buildings have been replaced by unfamiliar ones; we're all having to get used to other people's taste and choices.

Our way of coping has been to project the positive over the negative and to appreciate that many people have faced natural disasters, survived and moved forward before us. We are by no stretch of the imagination unique. The tsunamis and earthquakes that hit the Pacific region in 2009 struck an extremely raw nerve; knowing intimately what those affected will be facing in two months, six months, a year, when the initial shock has worn off, gives such news bulletins a different edge now. The stark reality is that our surroundings have changed forever: you either walk away from that or set about creating a new environment, whether collectively or individually, or both.

I hope somebody is writing a manual on how to cope with the environmental changes following a natural disaster. Perhaps some wise counselling in this regard might convince more people to stay.

9

A nation's generosity

ALMOST immediately following the fires, we heard reports of the generosity that was flowing, seemingly non-stop. The first trickle of vital goods and emergency payments was all we could focus on and it was many weeks before it dawned that what was coming into our local emergency centres had turned into an avalanche of furniture, clothing, household goods, toiletries and more. The main depot at Whittlesea had been expanded to house it all, and more local centres were established in Kinglake, Pheasant Creek, Flowerdale, St Andrews, Hurstbridge and Yarra Glen. On top of all this, millions of dollars were pouring into the Red Cross Appeal Fund that was set up on 8 February: more than $379 million was eventually transferred to a state government trust account for distribution. At that stage, we had no notion of how such funds would be allocated, but assumed that the most needy—the uninsured, families, the elderly, injured, ill and disabled—would take priority.

There were also phenomenal efforts by individuals, volunteers and not-for-profit organisations. Their offerings were, in many cases, including our own, just what was needed at the right time— often small gestures but with a huge personal impact: a bag of bulbs to plant on a devastated block for spring; warm, waterproof coats for our dogs, sewn by a stranger; even books to replenish lost home libraries—this was special soul food, since books weren't on the list of necessary goods.

My first day back at work, on Monday 16 February, revealed a microcosm of what had been inspired in the wider community. My colleagues had raised a considerable sum of money and with it purchased thoroughly practical gift vouchers for things such as clothes and day-to-day items; the company had also put money in my bank account. Others had brought in items of clothing and cooking appliances; one anonymous person left an envelope of cash at the reception desk. Once again, it was a very strange feeling to be the beneficiary of other people's generosity.

Sean had the same experience in his workplace, his colleagues having raised a considerable amount of cash. They, like my workmates, had spent a horrified weekend watching the events unfold, knowing our family was in the middle of it. These things always happen to somebody else: it was now close to home, personal, and they reacted in the most generous and thoughtful way. Rather than contributing to the community appeal fund, they decided to help the person they knew. It was months before we used those vouchers, which we filed away until we were capable of more rational decision-making and also could organise storage. We felt absolutely compelled to exchange the vouchers for goods that truly meant something.

Other friends took the same approach. When we'd decided what we needed, they would buy it for us or keep it until we were ready. We still couldn't quite articulate our requirements to anyone close, so they'd take the initiative: turn up with plants, lend a caravan, put aside some clothes or surplus furniture, arrive with a wheelbarrow or tools, give their time and skills to help with the barn fit-out. Sean's daughter, Claire, arrived with an amazing collection of bedding, cookware and skincare products donated by Myer, where she works. It's what friends and family do and we'd do exactly the same if the circumstances were reversed.

For us, there was incalculable value in the replacement of goods such as tools and fencing. Sean can turn his hand to most things, but the complete lack of even a screwdriver and hammer, not to mention power tools, made these a logistical and financial priority. All due respect to the tradesmen of the world, but with our own tools we knew could save a small fortune. Lions Clubs mobilised to amass shovels, garden gear and general tools that would at least get people going.

I've already mentioned Blaze Aid, which was for us a stunning example of Australians' generosity and can-do spirit. But it was about more than posts and wire: these people were a practical salve for the soul and whenever their crews were working on our property I felt an overwhelming sense of relief and admiration. The volunteers included elderly, retired farmers from far north Queensland, couples, people who had been laid off from jobs, young intellectually disabled people, and the inspiring team leader Craig, who got it all rolling. And they came not only from all over Australia but from across the world: there were New Zealanders, Swiss, English, Argentinians, Canadians, Americans and Austrians—all sweet, generous, self-sufficient.

The 2700 or so volunteers constructed 400 kilometres of fencing on seventy properties. After eight months, Blaze Aid had to wind up, as the volunteers fell away and the organisers got back to running their own properties and businesses. But all of the tools that were donated to them have been safely stored away and will come out when the next bushfire disaster demands it. As a community, a state and a nation, we can't put a value on the love and labour provided by those people.

In our confused state in the immediate aftermath of the fires, we weren't up to giving the larger financial implications any sensible consideration, let alone realistically calculating what our needs were. At the same time, I seemed to fix on smaller-scale money matters. I recall, on our second trip off the mountain to Whittlesea, ringing the phone company to pay a bill I knew had been in the house. There was also a credit card that had become overdue: I was frantic about this, since we always pay the full amount by the due date and resent accruing any interest.

Many organisations, including phone companies and banks, announced that they were suspending payments due from bushfire victims; power companies were working out the time people had been without electricity and would recalculate all bills. But the fact was that these debts weren't going to go away—at the end of whatever period of moratorium was offered, there'd be a mountain of catch-up requirements. Keeping track of it all was likely to be a bit of a mind-bender for our still-addled brains, so we wanted to clear debts as they arose and avoid nasty future surprises. We became a little fanatical about not having any financial matters outstanding, or any borrowed goods that had to be kept track of.

It was several months before we began to receive correspondence outlining our expected entitlements from the Bushfire Appeal Fund in the wake of our losses. The magic piece of paper was a Department of Human Services 'green form' that included a registration number indicating whether you'd been totally destroyed, partially destroyed or not destroyed. It was the key to material-aid centres and the number to quote for any claims, and remains the key form of survivor identification. The green form became a much-handled and tatty document in a short space of time and was subsequently replaced with a laminated card.

One of the most frequently asked questions, almost from the time money began to be dispensed, was whether it was going in the right direction—being used for what it was intended for—and whether people were able to handle the influx of large sums. It is a fair thing to ask, but I can't see how such a distribution can be audited or moral judgements be made about personal decisions on how it should be spent. The total amounts received by individuals can cause an intake of breath—until, that is, you start to calculate what it costs to build a life from ground zero upwards.

The first payment was an emergency grant from Centrelink for up to $10 000 for a family or $7000 for a couple or individuals in the fire-affected areas. In our case, it went into our bank account and was used for immediate necessities; to this day, I couldn't give a detailed accounting of how it was spent, but the amounts for even basic items such as underwear and a modest new handbag, since I couldn't get the smell of bushfire smoke out of my original one, soon added up. In addition to publicly raised funds such as those from the Red Cross Bushfire Appeal, there were also charitable offerings from rural organisations, services clubs and a vast array of community-minded groups. It was announced in March that owners whose principal place of residence had been totally destroyed would receive a $50 000 payment from the Bushfire Appeal Fund, whether they were insured or not, and there would be no means testing. We got our fair share of 'Wow, you're doing all right out of this' comments as soon as it hit the news. Insured and still copping a lump sum like that! Such throwaway lines made us feel guilty and embarrassed, compelled to somehow justify our situation. Again, we hadn't by then made any final decisions about how we would use the money, so it remained in the bank until we were ready to place official orders for the barn project.

Material aid also continued to pour by the truck-load into each of the local relief centres. Free-meal venues sprang up, along with the first stopgap army tents for those who had been left homeless. Aid agencies doled out supermarket and petrol vouchers or cash for people who were struggling to make ends meet. Some of the material-aid centres were still there after eight months. For us, they were a fabulous first reclothing resource, but we were travelling very light while living with others and had no desire to acquire extraneous 'stuff' that had to be stored. Was the aid system rorted, were there people who took advantage of public sympathy and generosity? Sadly, the short answer is yes, some did. Eventually a number limit was placed on certain items, after people were seen taking goods away by the trailer-load. We would look on, bemused, as a large load of dog food was hauled down the road; cars were filled to their rooftops with pallets of bottled water; tools were almost fought over.

While there are unique aspects to the Black Saturday experience, previous bushfire events, such as Ash Wednesday, had lessons to teach us about the impact of charity on affected communities, such as neighbours resenting neighbours, and those who were uninsured obviously battling to regroup their finances in order to rebuild to the same level as previously. The distribution of anything 'free' invariably raises the thorny issue of equitable decision-making. Who deserves what? Are some more deserving than others? What circumstances are taken into account? Where does means testing come in? From my observations, once the aid started to flow the diviseness inherent in such charitable handouts began to emerge. As we knew well from firsthand experience, some people seemed to assume that those who had suffered a total property loss and received all of the so-far-available grants from the Bushfire Appeal Fund were, as a result, rolling in financial clover.

There were whispers from those who felt some entitlement but were excluded from claiming. The insidious rumour mill targeted people who had supposedly splashed their grant money on new cars they could never have afforded previously, or on a ritzy new house to replace their modest, old weatherboard; someone who took off on a luxury holiday; people who quit jobs. Who knows what anyone's personal financial circumstances were before and after the fires? If anyone had compared my modest replacement car with the brand-new, fully optioned sporty number that sat in our driveway beforehand, the assumption would have been that we hadn't had insurance. On the contrary, the cost-effective vehicles Sean and I chose to replace what we had lost were simply our most sensible economic options. But assumptions and badly drawn conclusions are a fact in affected communities and can be extremely disruptive.

One particular bone of contention (though not, I hasten to add, as far as friends and family were concerned) were the larger, publicly raised grants. Entitlements for those who'd lost loved ones were never at issue—for children without parents, for parents who'd lost children, or for those facing lengthy, ongoing medical treatment—and indeed it struck me and others that these particular grants were a little slow in coming. There was another basic criterion for eligibility: namely, that the destroyed or damaged property had to be clearly identified as the principal place of residence.

Business grants also came in for their share of scrutiny: who got them and why, who qualified and who didn't, why some people were apparently knocked back while others with part-time enterprises received the full amounts. But the greatest public attention has understandably been reserved for the Bushfire Appeal Fund grants. Soon after the initial $50 000 was announced, a further payment of up to $40 000 was rolled out; this one was stringently means-tested, and granted on a sliding scale of need. Along with many others, we didn't qualify. Nor did we apply for it as such: the paperwork filled out for the first $50 000 formed the basis for qualification for any subsequent grants, so notification of what was or wasn't coming your way was automatic. The intention was, in my book, fair: families with school-age children, pensioners and those with other dependants were going to find the financial road ahead particularly tough. Besides, charities such as the Red Cross are above all about helping people in need. (The test was later modified and the criteria revisited, with the result that every owner of a totally destroyed primary place of residence again received some money.)

But each individual views need differently. Arguments arose about whether people who had lost holiday homes, weekenders and investment properties were deserving of grant money. Some people who'd lost infrastructure but still had a house standing voiced their feeling that they'd been somehow cheated. Some small rural holdings qualified for grants; others that came in just under the number of hectares required for eligibility missed out. Charity groups began to work more on a word-of-mouth basis to distribute what they had to offer. It had become apparent early on that some people were persistently accessing the free services and monetary grants, while others totally eschewed them. That's human nature, of course, and shouldn't come as a shock.

What disaster-affected people place greatest value on is, like anything else, going to vary from individual to individual. Sean and I felt morally obliged in regard to the fund money that came our way, all of which we earmarked for rebuilding and restoring some value to our land. Even an additional $2000 winter handout for people shivering in temporary accommodation, which became known as the 'blanket grant', was used to buy insulation for the temporary living section we installed in the barn. Without the Bushfire Appeal Fund grants, we wouldn't have been able to build the barn so easily, but even so, the main structure wasn't entirely covered by what we received and we accomplished the fit-out through careful use of our own funds and some savvy recycling. The furnishings came from friends and family, or welfare agencies.

The material-aid handouts continued unabated through most of 2009, but the question is whether they remained relevant all that time. Undoubtedly the goods saved families a lot of money on shopping bills along the way, but after the first few months we found the notion of calling into the centres strange. What for—another tube of toothpaste or a toilet roll? We knew we would, though, need some good secondhand items once we moved into the barn, as furnishing temporary accommodation with expensive new stuff just isn't practical. Some agencies, such as the Salvation Army, realised it was important for donations to be staggered to meet needs as they arose, and kept funding in reserve for that purpose.

Like many others, it was practical goods that we appreciated most. Once people moved into temporary accommodation or got a house built, case workers ensured there were fridges, washing machines, beds or a pack of kitchen items, which seemed to roll up the driveway on a Salvos truck at exactly the right moment. When compassion fatigue sets in, which it inevitably does at some stage after a disaster, is the time when survivors are most in need. Often they get by with very little at first, but eventually they need to face having to acquire at least the basic goods to make a house liveable. In our case, after seven months of living with John and Julie we had no need for a moving van to get our worldy goods back to Number 59. But within a week or two we needed core furniture and items such as cookware and crockery, and storage solutions for clothes. For us, the shipping container had been worth its weight in gold for storing such things until we needed them, but not everybody in a disaster zone has such an option available.

There were so many groups and individuals whose generosity went above and beyond the call of duty too. The support from the RSPCA was stunning. They provided stockfeed and pet supplies by the truck-load, specialised veterinary services were put in place rapidly, and they built new horse shelters for many people, including us.

I felt compelled to track down the people in uniform who had been so big-hearted and helpful to us. Senior Sergeant Dan Trimble, the police officer who took Harley off the mountain and helped get him to a vet in time, was stunned when he received our letter of thanks. He hadn't received too many of those in his career, because both he and the public figured he was just doing his job. But as a member of the first response team to come into Kinglake, what he had driven into that night was about as tough as an assignment gets, yet he used his own time to save our precious, suffering dog. And the vet refused to charge us a cent for the phenomenal ongoing care Harley received.

Along the way there have also been additional donations, including holidays for jaded survivors, or a small army of friends and volunteers potting up plants for the garden or giving up weekends to help with the barn fit-out. Then there were the craft groups that churned out beautiful handmade gifts, from an endless supply of colourful wool beanies to a stunning patchwork quilt that was delivered to us and has already become a family treasure. Corporates rolled out vouchers and household goods, which again were sensibly delayed until people most needed them and were distributed on a point-score basis to ensure fairness.

The appeal fund was closed to donations on 17 April; by mid-October it had distributed $321 million. At the time of writing, there was still a great deal of money being held by the fund, which has been earmarked for community building projects rather than any further individual survivor grants. There is already a growing sense of hostility towards any attempts to use it for programs that would normally be expected to be funded by local, state or federal governments. The fund has stated that this won't be the case, but until communities can regroup, both finding out who represents their needs and applying for these funds will continue to play out over time.

At the end of the day, the fund is answerable to the vast number of people who dug deep to create it, and the public deserves a voice in how it should be spent from here on in. But the sooner there is an end to it then, I believe, the sooner communities can settle down. And as for whatever is left in material-aid warehouses and distribution centres, they can ship our share to other recent victims of natural disasters in our region, such as Samoa and Indonesia.

10

'Trauma brain'

Many people, including your nearest and dearest, are often too polite to constantly ask how you might be travelling emotionally after a major traumatic event. They understand when you inadvertently forget birthdays, miss appointments and burble on disconnectedly about personal issues in the middle of a conversation about something totally unrelated. It is thoughtful and accommodating of them, though it must be said that there are times when a bit of a wake-up call—an indicator that you aren't behaving normally—would be useful.

There is no shortage of literature about dealing with post-traumatic stress, but the bottom line is to remain alert to signs that something might not be fully connecting in the neuron department. Symptoms and behaviours that we had experienced during the fires lingered on for some time afterwards. A full night's sleep continued to elude us for months. A stretch of four hours was a luxury, whereas I'd normally be non-functional with less than eight, though this didn't seem to impact on our physical or mental energy levels in the initial stages. At times we resorted to excessive 'self-medication' in an effort to relax, but alcohol didn't touch the proverbial sides—no effect whatsoever. The same went for tranquillisers and sleeping tablets. The psyche had its own ideas and stayed in a constant state of high alert for six months; any sleep I did get was dreamless. Even now, some nights I wake up in the early hours of the morning for no apparent reason and wander about aimlessly until exhaustion takes over.

The timeless sensation we'd all experienced during and immediately after the fires also continued for months. It was a battle to keep track of times and dates, which may well have been a side-effect of sleep deprivation. If you'd asked us what we did the day before, or even that morning, we simply couldn't remember. Yesterday had been expunged and tomorrow was too far away—we took things one day at a time.

The other source of frustration was an inability to think clearly, to finish sentences or a train of thought; engaging in daily conversation took a concentrated effort. Straightforward day-to-day tasks—going to the supermarket or the bank, organising some paperwork—would fall victim to an indecisive fog. I would find myself standing in a shop, completely blank, wondering what I was doing there. Several times, in the supermarket, I left my half-full trolley and just walked out. Even a shopping list didn't seem to register: there was no connection between the items on it and what I was looking at on the shelves. On Julie's first trip to the super-market, she told us when she got home that she'd walked through the checkout like a robot without putting her purchases on the counter to be scanned. Aha, I thought, it's not just me. Attempts to acquire necessities—clothes, hair products, shoes—were equally unsuccessful. What I was observing, trying to choose from, just didn't seem right, so mostly I'd make no decision at all. Even now, impulse buying seems to have gone out the window; what I might once have bought because it was attractive or a bit different is now dismissed as unnecessary or frivolous.

The tricky part is sifting through the 'guidebook' and deciding which part of your behaviour is to be expected, is normal some-how, and what are the telltale signs that a day of feeling down is in danger of plummeting into a more extended period of the blues. It took me months to recognise and deal with certain personal actions and reactions, and that is, in fact, still an issue. Getting through the initial days hour by hour turned into getting through the weeks day by day, assuming you were doing fine because you'd made it to the weekend without a meltdown. The sense of humour is intact, we're functioning, feeling quite strong and planning a future. Situation pretty normal, really.

What we hadn't fully anticipated, though, was the cumulative effect of successive extraordinary experiences. We came to know this state of mind as 'trauma brain': one thought at a time, one decision at a time (and, even then, a spontaneous one), the avoidance of multiple choices. We would pore over money decisions endlessly, whereas previously they were fairly cut and dried. Running into a brick wall with a service provider, dealing with any sort of incompetence, could reduce us to rage—or, just as easily, to despair. Even tuning into television or radio and trying to absorb 'heavy' issues has taken time. News related to our circumstances, the forming of a royal commission, major political issues, the machinations of the local shire council—any of which would once have got us steamed up—ceased to matter much. If it didn't directly relate to getting through the day, it could be ditched.

Similarly, small talk, people complaining about seemingly selfish things, idiotic drivers, or thoughtless comments and actions, tended to take on monumental proportions. It was as if we'd been asked to assess in detail what information we really needed and what was surplus to requirements. Even now, there is no flicking on of television or radio just for the sake of it, and if a program bores us or is inconsequential we talk instead.

Trauma was, of course, also a reality for our extended family. They too had suffered a loss and felt a need to grieve, while at the same time keeping a watchful eye on us for any signs of aberrant behaviour. Our closest friends and family found it incredibly hard to visit us for some time after the fires, and all of them were reduced to tears when first faced with the obliteration of a place that held so many happy memories. Other friends got as far as John and Julie's, but couldn't bring themselves to cross the road to Number 59.

But we cherished their encouragement, the praise for every step forward, the sensible advice and the practical help when needed. Typical of this was arriving home to find our dear friend Camille had simply turned up to do some planting. 'I knew you'd say not to get dirty and it's all a dangerous mess. So I decided not to wait for an invitation, just had to get something back in the ground,' she said. She'd also loaded her car with a bottle of wine and some cheese and biscuits, which we shared in the trusty caravan. Things like that—positive, thoughtful, genuine—touch you deeply.

Overall, we felt fortunate that we were travelling through the recovery process without any major crashes, so far. Among the survivors there had been reports of suicides, relationship breakdowns, people still in serious denial, ongoing grieving, anxious children, enormous isolation for those forced away from their communities, and feelings of injustice and abandonment.

In many instances, it has been the support of others in the community that has helped people through. In the early stages of our barn-building project, Sean and I were working to clear felled trees at Number 59 when a car pulled up. Out jumped Lorrie Casey, the friend John and I had met on the main road on the night of the fire, with her old dog Sheba. We'd been searching in vain for Lorrie ever since, concerned about what had happened to her. This was the first time she'd toured the neighbourhood. 'I'll go and get us some lunch at the bakery. I really need to have lunch with somebody,' she said, roaring off and soon returning with a selection of hot pies, including one each for the dogs, and a six-pack of beer.

Lorrie hadn't yet returned to her own property; instead, she said, she'd come up the mountain at weekends and sit in what used to be a scenic reserve off the main road, trying to summon the courage to face her blitzed home. 'There's no time like the present,' Sean said, and took her there to see whether we could get a container in place. When they returned, we swapped notes about the joys of shipping containers, finding good builders, and staying on the mountain. Lorrie yearned to come back, but couldn't get her head around the enormity of the task on her own.

'When John and I ran into you on the road that night, what on earth had happened?' I asked her. She had no recollection of having seen or spoken to us: her entire focus was on her friend and neighbour, the CFA volunteer, lying badly burnt on the back seat of her car. When the fire threat escalated that day, Lorrie's neighbour asked her to come and get her dog as she'd been given the choice of staying to defend her property or joining the crew on the fire truck. She stayed, but wanted the dog taken to safety. Lorrie had barely made it back to her place when the firestorm barrelled over the hill and sent her fleeing to the township for her life. Then her neighbour called again, asking that she take care of the dog since she didn't expect to make it out alive. Lorrie reacted instinctively, driving back through the fire, smoke and chaos before being stopped by a fallen tree. She left her car running and found her neighbour fighting for her life. Lorrie got her to safety and she was taken off the mountain by air ambulance. After that night Lorrie had slept for a week in her car, with the two dogs. Once her neighbour was released from hospital, the two women began sharing a rental house off the mountain while working hard to find a way to get back again. She described to us the symptoms with which we were all too familiar: the sleeplessness, the disjointed thought patterns, the sense of disconnection and, some days, the struggle just to function.

Other friends relayed their experiences of nursing victims through the night after they'd crawled out of burning cars, or of seeing neighbours on fire. Where there is a disaster with a large death toll, stories such as these abound and are part of a collective, wider experience. You can either deal with the ongoing fact of horror piled on horror, much of it revealed many months after the event, or go into some sort of denial.

So, is the answer to get help, to work it all through with a professional? For some survivors, that was the case and they have found enormous comfort and healing in the psychological and counselling services offered by the state and federal governments. There was, however, something of a one-size-fits-all approach to these services in the interim stages—quite understandable, given the enormity and urgency of the task. We were all going to get a case manager, but what sort of case manager would be most appropriate for the individual took months to identify. The focus was on emotional dealing and healing—name a natural stress-relieving therapy and it was on tap—but what Sean and I craved more was a clear brain that could access the services most valuable to us, keep us updated and carry out practical functions such as determining barn-building requirements or chasing them through. We did, though, resort to free massage and relaxation sessions in the hope they would restore that elusive sleep.

In our deep-rooted self-sufficiency, we found dealing with strangers as personally confronting as standing in a Centrelink queue. Even the notion of being automatically appointed a case manager was difficult to comprehend and, besides, much of what we were feeling was difficult to articulate to outsiders. In reality, Sean and I had formed our own counselling circle with John and Julie, talking ad nauseam about our shared experience, finding this easier than trying to describe it to others. We even developed our own post-traumatic humour and language, laughter often proving the best leveller when something became psychologically or personally sticky.

Nonetheless, whether your property was totally destroyed, partially destroyed, or not touched but in a fire-affected community, a case manager went with the territory. Given the scale of the task—seventy-eight communities were affected by the fires, and some 3400 properties damaged or destroyed—initial case managers were drawn from any source the state and federal governments could raid: some came from private welfare services, others from federal government programs. What they walked into must have been incredibly difficult.

The first one appointed to us was extremely nice and eager to help, but as a youth outreach worker he wasn't perhaps the greatest fit. And even while he was trying to get his head around our plight, he was still trying to deal with drug-affected kids at railway stations. 'You'll probably end up counselling him!' Tania joked. He did his best to help us access services, but what we felt we needed most was an extra pair of arms and legs. Another couple we met revealed that they'd had six different case workers and still didn't have a handle on where to go to next. Others had silently stopped accessing theirs when they left the mountain, whether temporarily or for good.

Then, via a circuitous route and with a tinge of 'It's not what you know, but who you know', we were connected with Bernadette Aylward. The Kinglake case management team leader, she'd been staying four nights a week with our friend Gretha Edwards in Steels Creek to be closer to 'the coalface'. In a heartbeat, 'No-bullshit Bernadette' figured out what we would and wouldn't tolerate, when she should and shouldn't intrude, what we needed the most and when to just roll in and check us out and share a laugh. Bernadette would dangle weekend getaways under our noses 'just in case', though she knew we wouldn't be diverted from our targets for achieving temporary accommodation. 'I'll call by for a cuppa' was her way of making sure we weren't just cracking tough. But most of all, she never patronised us or did other than credit us with the ability to handle our lives. She knew we'd whistle loudly if we needed to. And we did need to, at which times she spent days chasing down a building permit, sourcing a portable bathroom/toilet arrangement to get us back on the block sooner, turning up to greet fencing volunteers, and organising to have vital goods delivered when we needed them. Turning up with a freshly knitted scarf and beanies on a cold day was another of her habits.

It would be a tall order to find a Bernadette for every survivor; they don't stamp too many out of that mould. Away from her own family for weeks at a stretch, she would sit in our freezing caravan and tick off a practical list of things she'd done for us. I jokingly came to refer to her as 'Saint Bernadette', but it wasn't all that far off the mark. The weight she took off our shoulders and the extent to which she restored our faith in the system have been phenomenal; we have never felt like a number since she's been in our orbit. Even being able to offload some vitriol to a neutral party has been a huge relief.

The cold, wet autumn and winter following the fires brought another challenge: we were constantly ill with bout after bout of flu—the worst flu I can remember experiencing—despite having been vaccinated. All four of us succumbed at some point, and as one of us began to recover another would go down for a fortnight;

we ran sick shifts to keep the household going. It played havoc with the psyche as well as the body: What's wrong with me? Am I finally cracking up? We endlessly analysed whether what we'd been breathing in since February—the arsenic from burning fences, the melted plastic and rubber, the diesel, gas and God knows what else—had seriously impaired our immune systems.

Then, in the middle of all this, we received a call to say our beloved horse Eliza was also ill. We rushed to where she was agisted, to find her scrabbling on the ground with terrible colic; she hadn't eaten for days. We summoned an emergency vet, who pronounced her in extreme pain and the colic terminal, with euthanasia the only possible course of action. We sat beside our beautiful Clydesdale, stroking her face and trying to talk her into getting up, but she'd been down too long and the effort was exhausting. Her best mate Ricky was frantic, pacing the fence beside her, practically screaming. It took a long time for the young vet to find a vein and administer the fatal dose. Even the earth-moving contractor we'd called to help us with the burial sat on the bobcat with tears in his eyes: 'That's too bloody awful to watch.' It was our first fatality and it wrung us emotionally dry. Ricky too was inconsolable, thrashing and screaming; we couldn't even think of floating him out until he was calm enough to handle.

Once back at John and Julie's, we went through the worst personal time we'd had since the fires. It was as though we'd let Eliza down, and her loss became a crisis point of guilt, grief, anger and disbelief. Bernadette called the RSPCA, who organised to have

Ricky housed elsewhere until we finished the fences and he could come home. According to the RSPCA's 2009 annual report, a major insight they gained from the fires was how much surviving animals meant to their owners: 'For many people who had lost so much, their animals were one of the few remaining reminders of their life before the bushfires and they took on even greater importance in their lives.' The RSPCA estimates that around one million animals died in the fires.

The RSPCA findings were confirmed again not long afterwards. We were in the process of moving goods between John and Julie's and the barn, and Jazz would trot between the two with us, often getting bored halfway through and taking herself back for a nap. One Sunday morning I assumed she'd gone with Sean, and vice versa: it soon became apparent that she was missing. Not ones to wonder, we snapped into search mode. Julie and I spent hours scouring every nook and cranny we could think of. At the end of the day we came up with nothing and I was inconsolable. Another lost animal was just too much to deal with; the tears didn't stop flowing. We leapt to the horrible conclusion that somebody had picked her up. We'd heard stories of dogs being picked up in bushfire zones and taken hundreds of kilometres before being handed in; people had assumed a solo pet was lost.

On the Monday morning, poor Bernadette copped a sobbing 'case', as did the RSPCA. A few weeks earlier we'd offered Jazz, Harley and Meg to the RSPCA to be photographed as bushfire survivors for any fundraising efforts they could use them for.

Jazz's photo was emailed to us in an instant and a small 'Find Jazz' army was mobilised; Bernadette drafted other case workers to ring animal shelters as well. Then the call came. 'There's a female Jack Russell cross at the RSPCA shelter in Epping,' she said. We emailed her photo and the shelter confirmed that they thought it was Jazz they had in custody, and Sean left work at lunchtime to get her. Epping is 40 kilometres away, quite a journey for a small, non-wandering dog. We'll never know how she came to be there, but an ambulance crew had picked her up and taken her to the shelter with the express instructions that if her owner wasn't found then one of them would take her. I felt weak with relief. Coming on top of our loss of Eliza, this had just about tipped me over the edge, providing another layer to that cumulative trauma. Then, for the icing on the cake, John decided to erect a makeshift roof over the back door. He was worried about me smoking cigarettes out there when it rained, fearing it might lead to another round of flu. But the scorched soil and grass had somehow been fused by the rain into a glass-like surface, and carrying in building materials one day John slipped and smashed his ankle. It took eight weeks of plaster, X-rays and immobility to restore his foot—it still gives him pain, which in turn causes me recurring guilt.

One thing the fires have done is make us more aware of certain types of human behaviour—the worst as well as the best. For example, we came across people who drew on the slimmest of associations to claim some part in others' very real loss—the 'I know somebody who knows somebody who knew people who died in the fires' thing, mostly from people not present in the community on that day and with only a remote or tenuous link. We came to cynically refer to this syndrome as 'trauma envy'.

Then there was a certain type of 'tourist'. That people wanted to pay homage or to spend some money in the town was something residents understood and gratefully acknowledged. But the flip side of the coin was insensitive 'rubber-necking', which could be the last straw for grieving people. Weekends turned into a nightmare of not being able to park outside the supermarket to get a bottle of milk; for weeks there was a traffic jam onto and off the mountain. We were aware of the arguments about reopening communities in order to get businesses up and running again, but every time there was talk of lifting the roadblocks I found myself on the edge of extreme panic. For me and many others, the closed community was a great comfort. People needed to be left in peace, to have time to regroup. We couldn't even bury our dead for several months, because of coronial requirements, and the thought of strangers scrambling through the ruins was chilling.

Signs went up on properties: 'Please, no photos.' People had died in some of these houses—who could want a happy snap of somebody else's tragic rubble in the family album? Yet, unbelievably, it was common to see strangers posing beside burnt-out properties. On one trip to the township I saw some children being photographed picking up the flowers that locals kept refreshed at one sad location, the flowers subsequently being slung uncereminiously on the grass. It made me feel sick and sorrowful for the rest of the day. We lost track of the people who walked up our drive to take photographs, and sometimes what they wanted was a souvenir, something charred.

The ravages of winter, both physical and psychological, began to abate a little as spring arrived. At least we could see some progress on the ground, and the emotional burden was becoming lighter. But we have no idea how we will cope with the height of summer. Survivors of Ash Wednesday have told us that the first anniversary is a raw time, as is the first day when conditions mirror those that brought the destruction. How will we feel when the weather bureau predicts temperatures over 40°C and a howling northerly? We won't know until we live it.

My granddaughter Carissa hates hearing about coming fire threats, the new warning systems, and she asks constantly whether it will be worse this time round. We just don't have an answer.

11

Going home

MOVING back to Number 59 on 31 August was cause for celebration. It was almost seven months since Black Saturday and the pull of being on our own land again was overwhelming, almost visceral. We had the barn up and a concrete floor, but not much else. It didn't matter, though: we had shelter and could make greater progress by being on the spot. It called for a special effort to be made for dinner and a good bottle of wine to toast the homecoming. Having never used a portable convection oven to any great extent, it was going to be hit-and-miss, but on went lime and coriander chicken and it was left to its own devices while we set up some minimal furniture.

We started our 'new life' with the caravan now parked inside the barn and one of those portable loos that caravanners cart around with them—really just a glorified potty with a lid and requiring some gymnastic maneouvres to get used to. But it was a five-minute drive to the communal shower and laundry facility that had been set up for people like us. We hooked up extension leads to a temporary power board on a pole in the garden.

During the previous week we'd transferred most of our goods from John and Julie's, and we simply announced on 31 August that we'd be moving into the barn that night. We knew John would protest and we were right; he was mortified, having envisaged a more gradual move. He feared that we were swapping Number 48 comfort for Number 59 hell because we felt we'd outstayed our welcome. 'What brought this on? It's too soon, things aren't fully ready over the road yet, it's too cold, has something gone wrong?' he protested. We reassured him that there was only one motive: we just had to do it, setting (and sticking to) a date to move back in was imperative to 'moving on'—the longer you are away, the easier it is to avoid the daunting task that lies ahead, to slide into the mindset that it's all too hard. If we waited until every glitch and inconvenience was ironed out, we'd still be in limbo. 'But I'm going to miss you,' John said. We all laughed at that one, given that we were a few minutes across the road.

That first night, while the chicken was ticking over, we jumped in the car to check out the shower facilities. I had on a pair of pyjama pants, ugg boots and a hoodie. 'Be just my luck to get pulled over by the police,' I said to Sean. There were a few little surprises—like the hot water that came through a very small instantaneous system and cut out before I'd even got wet, and the bitterly cold gale that whistled under the door and slapped the clammy shower curtain around my goose-bumped body. Sean suggested I try the men's shower block, but I passed on that for fear that some hapless male would walk in. I made it back home, my wet hair wrapped in a towel, without bumping into any neighbours—not that they would care, but my personal dignity was taking enough of a battering.

The communal laundry was a godsend in the early stages. It was, though, a little confronting to find all our gear folded beautifully by an anonymous volunteer from a church group that would descend and perform such chores. They even folded the underwear! (Sean began to refer to them as his 'holy undies'.) It became a bit of a contest to collar an empty dryer, but we remembered that our stash from the spa man included a fold-up clothesline, which Sean installed on a wall of the barn. It was something I had long hankered after: an indoor clothesline, not dependent on the weather. And it left dryers free for the small army of women with young children, whose destroyed laundries had previously gone non-stop to keep up with the load. We had a donated secondhand washing machine stashed in the container, but it would be some time until we'd have the plumbing to get it working. Compared to those young mums, though, we didn't have a problem.

In addition, we were seasoned campers—over the years we'd lived out of the back of our Land Rover in some very remote and rugged holiday locations—and that experience helped enormously. Plus there were just the two of us. It made my heart ache when we'd pass young families trying to coexist in caravans, converted containers or portable classrooms. It takes a lot of guts to deal with that. At the same time, our circumstances now were not as romantic as those camping trips had been—digging a hole in your own garden doesn't quite have the same appeal, and an attentive audience of two dogs didn't add to the experience.

But once the reality of being back on our block sank in, the temporary inconveniences fled and our sense of homelessness started to evaporate. We'd carefully inventoried what we needed to make the barn initially liveable and spent nights after work doing bits and pieces to fit it out accordingly; we knew it was crucial to accept that this was going to be an evolving process. We'd set up an outdoor table and chairs inside, turned a bookshelf donated by John and Julie into a makeshift open pantry, raided the shipping container for crockery, cutlery and cookware. We had the portable oven, an electric slow-cooker, a donated electric wok, and the caravan's gas cooktop. The appliances sat either on the concrete floor or on a low coffee table near the only power outlet. And there wasn't much we didn't manage to turn out of those limited appliances: great lamb shanks, pasta, roasts, stir-fries and even a batch or two of biscuits. For dishwashing, we'd fill the kettle from the tap on the water tank outside.

The Kinglake weather didn't let us down on our first night, offering seemingly endless gale-force winds. 'It's a pretty good building job,' Sean said. 'There's not a single squeak or creak in this structure.' That was heartening. What did shatter our peace, however, were gumnuts hitting the steel roof like bullets, some having been rendered diamond-hard by the fire. They and the odd flying twig reminded us that this was a shed built for tractors and machinery, not to house human beings. But we figured that eventually we could install some sort of insulation in the roof over the living section. We cheerfully dished up the chicken, poured the wine and watched two excited dogs check out their new abode; it was months since they'd been that close to scrounging something off the dinner table.

Sean couldn't contain his glee, sitting at the table rugged up in a heavy jacket, hood on and declaring: 'I can feel the stress draining away, just being able to sit back here in our own place.' Our attempts at extended conversation turned into helpless laughter when a downpour on the metal roof drowned out everything else. We couldn't hear ourselves think. After the initial pounding, the continuing run-off was like a waterfall as it hurtled off gutters and headed to the water-tank inlets. The cold wind barrelled through the gaps under the doors and where the roof met the walls, but we felt like a couple of kids who'd pitched a tent out on the back lawn. They were our sounds: we were in our own space again, under our own roof, and we revelled in it. Sean didn't stop chuckling proudly about having met his self-imposed deadline for our return.

With minimal light and no heating apart from a hot-water bottle and a small blow heater, there was nothing for it but to retreat to bed in the caravan. It was warm under the the pile of doonas and blankets, but not really a space designed for two adults, a hot-water bottle and a little terrier. Jazz has always been banned from the bedroom, but here she had no physical boundaries and a blast of warm air to boot, so up she jumped. Meg, on the other hand, was delighted just to have us constantly in sight and hunkered down on her hammock bed, snoring loudly. We only needed Harley to complete the scene, but he was still with Tania. The caravan bed had a round-ended mattress that made it difficult to keep our feet on board. Then there was the low overhead shelf and cupboards—sit up in a hurry or roll over for a stretch and whack! 'I can't believe people tow these bloody things around the countryside and call it a relaxing holiday,' I muttered to Sean. 'It's actually pretty comfortable,' he said. Then again, he could sleep on a concrete slab.

Thankfully, we had the luxury of knowing that we could progress to a more comfortable set-up in a short space of time. Others camping back on their land had nothing to park caravans in and so they bore the full brunt of the cold; getting through a freezing night became known as 'death by doona'. The trick for us was to keep focusing ahead and to realise just how little you can actually get by with. Apart from anything else, it doesn't take much to mess up a caravan: leave some clothes, shoes and toiletries lying about, a few dishes in the tiny sink and your laptop on the table, and it's chaos.

Another thing we had to learn was to not overload the power circuits. It didn't take much to do so. If we tried to run the TV, kettle, fridge and heater at the same time, we'd have a blackout.

There were no lights left burning unnecessarily at Number 59. For those who generate their own solar power and live off the grid, this is a fact of life, but for the novice it can take some practice. We also learned to be frugal in other ways. When water requires a dash outside in the cold and rain, recycling becomes a matter of course. Having been reliant on rainwater tanks for sixteen years, we thought we were pretty good at conserving water, but you can always learn new tricks. Actually being able to see your water supply dropping is a great catalyst for further frugality—we took to filling a 25-litre plastic container to save those cold, wet trips outside, and it became a challenge to see how far that quantity could stretch. Rather than washing just one or two coffee mugs we'd wait for a sinkload, and we re-used the contents of our hot-water bottle time after time.

The home comfort that pretty well everyone in temporary accommodation missed most was a some semblance of a 'bathroom'—in other words, an on-site toilet and shower. The ever-practical case manager Bernadette got the picture that this might help keep people on their land once they'd returned, and indeed for many it made the difference between giving camping a go and staying off the mountain; they'd put up with a battered tent as long as there was some sort of bathroom option. Trying to use communal facilities and get to work in a reasonable state wasn't easy: I'm a woman who can't handle not having my hair right, which meant going back to the caravan to attempt a blow-dry—not always successful.

Any future guidebook should advise that these facilities be incorporated sooner rather than later, once there's some basic infrastructure to support them. We could have been back home weeks earlier if that had been the case. Ironically, one night there was a piece on the radio highlighting the living conditions of refugees arriving in Australia. Some, it noted, were living in tents and caravans without toilet facilities, which just wasn't acceptable in a civilised country like Australia. This made me chuckle: the 'refugees' in Kinglake and the other fire-affected zones knew how they felt.

It was late September before a much-coveted portable shower and loo arrived courtesy of the state government. We've probably all used one at some point—at an outdoor function, rock concert, on a building site. Not beautiful, but it does the basic job. Ours was plonked on the supposedly level gravel outside the barn and hooked up to the water tank. A rubber hose carried the soapy effluvium to what used to be to part of the front garden, eventually drowning the emerging relict daffodils and snowdrops; every time it frothed out into open view, we had to question the hygiene angle. The doors afforded a great view across the top paddock, but also straight up Deviation Road: a loo with a view—every home should have one. But, of course, this worked in reverse too, and a driver on the road at the right moment would witness the bathrobed O'Connors picking their way across the gravel, destination obvious.

Sean road-tested the shower but wasn't a happy camper afterwards. 'It's been put on an uphill slope. Instead of the water going down the plughole, I'm in it up to my knees,' he railed. Still, when it came time to get ready for work, armed with towel and highlighting shampoo, in I went. There was nowhere to hang the towel, so I slung it out onto the gravel along with the bathrobe and ugg boots. 'The hot-water supply is limited, so don't muck around in there,' Sean yelled through yet another gale. As though we dedicated water conservationists 'muck around' under the shower anyway, but a shampoo and condition can be squeezed in. On it went, shampoo happening, then bang! The water stopped dead. Out I came, dripping, purple shampoo nicely frothed, retrieved the bathrobe and slippers and tore into the barn. 'Oh shit, it's blown the power,' Sean offered by way of explanation. 'I'll have to reset it.' While he did that, I resorted to the loo, freezing and still wet. As one particularly strong blast of Kinglake gale ripped the door open and sent it almost off its hinges, Murphy's law dictated that there would be a truck coming down the road! There was nothing to do but wave at the truck driver.

Soon after this, we heard via the bush telegraph that there was such a thing as a luxury portable ensuite that could be towed on-site like a trailer. The sort of deal the star would demand on an outback movie set—complete with vanity basin, porcelain loo, good shower, towel racks, heater, exhaust fan and robe hooks, and able to be plumbed into the septic system. Granted, it seemed a bit precious in our circumstances, but it would provide a blessed few weeks of breathing space before our own facilities could be installed. A week later it rolled through the door—ablution heaven on wheels.

It was around this time that Carissa felt ready to come and check out the barn. By now we had a few more facilities and Sean had bought a smaller version of one of those patio heaters provided outdoors by cafés when the weather turns cold. It took pride of place on the table, since the gas bottle could sit underneath and the supply be fed up through the umbrella hole. In the future we could use the heater outside on chilly spring and autumn nights.

Bernadette was checking on our progress regularly and I mentioned to her that I needed to buy a bed since Sean had laid the floor in the mezzanine area that was destined to become the new boudoir, and we wanted Carissa to be able to stay overnight. A few days later, a Salvation Army truck backed up the driveway with a new bed on board. They also unloaded a pack containing all those small kitchen things you don't know you've lost until you come to use them: potato peeler, can opener, tea-towels, strainer, cheese grater. Thank God for the Salvos—it was perfect timing.

It made sense to set up our new bed near the caravan, so Carissa could sleep in the caravan. Sean retrieved the piece of carpet we'd scored from the spa man and wheeled the bed onto it. Bliss! Something better than concrete for the feet to land on.

The 'headboard' was a Colorbond wall. On Carissa's first visit, she spent some time pacing out the barn floor, which of course stood above the old house site. 'Is this where my bedroom used to be? Where was the old kitchen?' She hunkered down in the caravan. 'It's like a cave in here; it's cool,' she decided. For Sean and me, having room to stretch in the bed was heaven. 'Thank God for the Salvos,' Sean repeated as he turned out the light.

But a few hours later we were both still tossing; my head felt as if it had been dipped in ice. 'The metal is sucking the heat out of our heads like a vacuum cleaner,' Sean explained. For some reason I found that immensely funny, along with his extended scientific rundown of heat exchange and lack of insulation. 'In other words we need a woolly hat,' I suggested. We crawled back into bed togged out in bright knitted beanies, which did the trick though they didn't add much in the way of glamour. 'I'll put up some sheets of chipboard tomorrow. A couple of those where our heads go will make all the difference,' offered my ever-practical, problem-solving husband.

The new ensuite was due to be installed in a few days' time, and all the gear from the house demolition was ready to go once the wall panels were up. Having only nights and weekends to do the work would make it all a very slow process, though, and it was exhausting to be, in effect, working round the clock. People badgered us to get away for a break, a rest and change of scenery, but until we had a workable living space that seemed like a remote proposition. We did the sums. Given that Sean could carry out the majority of the work needed, how would the figures stack up if he left his job for several months and completed the barn, instead of our having to call in tradesmen for every major project? It was no contest. Even with electricians, plumbers and builders to do the compliance-certificate work, we could do the rest ourselves for far less. We had no personal debt and could live frugally on one salary in the meantime.

By the end of September and a month into the barn process, it sometimes seemed that we had made little progress. But it wasn't long before the Barn Mahal started to turn into something of a tourist attraction: locals would remark on it, people would stop at the front gate and tradesmen would comment on how well it was coming together. We stopped feeling that we were somehow lagging behind and became stalwart about sticking to our schedule. Friends came to help and over one weekend we got the main wall panels in place. With a rapid undercoat of white paint, it started to look positively ritzy. Next, Patsy and Jimmy arrived to stay for a week, camping in their own caravan while they helped us get the outrageous designer kitchen back together. Suddenly we'd gone from an outdoor table and singed chairs to a workable oven, bench space and sink. Even with gas still to be connected to hotplates, and only moderate water pressure, we felt as though we'd moved from a tent to a palace.

As I write, the palace remains littered with building materials, power circuits are still to be completed to all areas and the mezzanine rooms haven't been fitted out. Our furniture is still trendily minimalist, which we felt was preferable to showering better items with endless sawdust. A lick of paint on some donated pieces and there is actually something resembling a decor. There are books and cookbooks back on shelves, suggesting that somebody really lives here and they read. A vase of flowers from our garden sits atop the fridge. 'Trust you to have to get that going on,' friend Patsy remarked. We have our own bathroom and it looks fantastic—spa bath, shower, easy-to-clean wall panelling, a big vanity basin, a huge mirror and cork tiles on the floor. Apart from those tiles, every fixture was recycled from the spa man. Sean has also started sealing the concrete floor in the living area. That should spell an end at last to constant concrete dust, not to mention deliver that funky warehouse-apartment look. It is now—almost—home.

12

Future tense

'I don't think people want to hear much more about the Black Saturday fires,' somebody remarked to me late in 2009. 'It's pretty much in the past now and everybody has sort of forgotten about it.' On another occasion, a delivery driver arrived unexpectedly with a pack of household goodies. When the driver walked into the barn, she couldn't contain her surprise: 'This is the first time I've been up here. I had no idea that people were still living in sheds—how awful for you after all this time. The people back at the office won't believe it.'

The human attention span is rather short, and it was ever thus. But for those who survived Australia's worst natural disaster, it will take years to settle into some new type of normal existence. The approach of the first anniversary of Black Saturday encouraged us to take stock and to look to the future—wallowing in the past doesn't endear you to anybody. In the same way, it's of little benefit to continue feeling disaffected about the fact that new, and hopefully better, approaches to fire safety have come too late for us—feeling somehow cheated is counter-productive. Rather, we hope those measures evolve well enough to save lives in the future.

For our personal circle, though, what is being done to prevent future loss of life and property has remained a key debating point. By the end of 2009, we began to take greater notice of the Bushfires Royal Commission findings and political pronouncements, albeit with some cynicism. One particularly valuable conclusion, at least as far we were concerned, was that communities such as ours were hit by the fires *before* appropriate warnings were issued. Some survivors have felt overwhelming guilt about not having somehow seen the fires coming, feeling they should not have been so complacent, should have educated themselves better. It was a huge slap in the face when, early in the commission hearings, some authorities remained adamant that fire warnings had gone out in time; it made those on the ground sound like liars. The fact is that we were on fire at 4.30 p.m., but heard constantly until 6.30 p.m. that we weren't affected. One of our neighbours sat in the Kinglake pub carpark ringed by fire and finally rang radio stations to tell them, before even the first ember alerts had been issued. Other parts of Kinglake didn't see flames until around 6 p.m., such was the random nature of that particular fire. That 'You should have known' guilt was only exacerbated by the comments of outsiders who rang radio stations to rail at these idiots who choose to live in the bush.

Many people have felt excluded from the Royal Commission: community meetings organised by the commission to determine the chief issues, and who should give evidence, were seen as something of a 'Take a number and we'll put you in a group session' token exercise. Most people didn't have the energy to dispute this perceived wrong, and decided in advance that there was going to be some sort of whitewash. As evidence continued to be heard, though, we regained some faith in the commission's preparedness to ask the tough questions. The new fire-warning scale established in 2009 was designed for the masses and distributed to all Victorians, but whether there is enough time for the messages to be fine-tuned only time will tell.

The endless evidence given in the Royal Commission about the inability of the fire services to work in unison or even communicate is a sad indictment on government inaction. But it is not surprising: having worked for one of those fire services a decade or so ago, all I can say is that nothing much appears to have changed. Much of the evidence has also made Ash Wednesday survivors very angry, revealing as it has that what came out of that disaster has still not been resolved twenty years later: fire refuges that didn't eventuate or were not maintained; seasonal burning-off that became bogged down in environmental arguments; the unrelenting advance of housing demand well beyond the city fringe.

The inevitable consequences of these failures are reflected in the tragic evidence of people who lost loved ones in the 2009 fires and in attempts to determine what caused the deaths: people attempting to flee too late; others staying with a house as they'd been led to believe it was the safest option under normal circumstances; fire bunkers that proved useless, as people couldn't get to them through the radiant heat; families who'd always said they'd leave on an extreme day instead following instructions to stay indoors and avoid clogging the roads with traffic.

The truth is that however many aerial water bombers or extra fire trucks had been enlisted, they could not have turned back the extreme, monstrous tide of Black Saturday. Once mother nature took over, the aircraft couldn't fly and the trucks couldn't get near the fire zones. Nor was there an easy explanation for the fact that certain properties burned and others with less fire-compliant features remained standing. We are closely studying new building codes, mandatory bushfire ratings, sprinkler systems and fire-fighting equipment: whether these can stave off fireballs that have the power of atom bombs can only be determined in the event.

In Kinglake's case, if it hadn't been for the dogged fundraising efforts of certain members of the community, there wouldn't even have been a decent fire station for hundreds of people to head towards that night. A few months ago, Sean and I went yet again to a large hardware store on a Sunday for building supplies. Parked down-wind of the sausage sizzle was the Kinglake fire tanker, each of its uniformed crew holding a fundraising tin. After all they'd been through, they were still giving up their weekends to help subsidise equipment and a new truck. Leading the crew was our neighbour Craig Lawless, his burnt face now healed and sporting his usual big smile. Several weeks later we attended a memorial service for his father Terry, who had succumbed to cancer. This man had spent twenty-five years either captaining the brigade or raising the funds to keep it going. He would have wondered 'What is all the bloody fuss about?' when half the community turned up to pay tribute to him. You could have heard a pin drop as a fire truck escorted the hearse off the mountain.

Another issue that has come under the spotlight is the fire levy and division of jurisdictional responsibilities between federal, state and local government during the fires, and how this was reflected in their actions, or in some cases inaction. Who steps in where? At what point are politics put aside in the interests of resurrecting ruptured communities? When does spin end and the greater good become paramount? That local government in fire-affected areas would struggle with the enormity of the situation wasn't too difficult to figure out, particularly as one shire council administered the majority of the burnt areas in the Great Dividing Range. But attempts to politicise any shortcomings in this respect will, I hope, be reflected at the ballot box next time round. Failure to operate in a coordinated way across municipal boundaries, refusal to access outside help or high-level expertise, and attempts to exclude community input have not been lost on the ratepayers. In addition, new buildings have gone up without proper approvals, sneaking in under the radar while the majority of a shattered community—incredibly time-poor as they combine work with rebuilding from scratch—didn't have the strength to object. In times like these, one would hope that the authorities could be trusted to truly represent the people's interests.

Many discussions are still to be had, even a year on. In future, at what point is the army brought in and what tasks should they perform? At what level of death and destruction is one overall point of command assigned? Who is in charge of the 'guide book' from now on, making sure it is updated, relevant and transparent? Who will cop the flak if road rage and panic lead to greater injury during a mass evacuation on inadedquate road systems when the first 'Catastrophic' fire warning is issued?

We are in for a nervous summer, and whichever state the next killer fire occurs in we will all be on a steep learning curve. The communities so devastated in 2009 have only, in the overall scheme of things, taken baby steps to recover. Sean and I, and John and Julie, have reconstituted our fire plans because once again we have chosen to stay. 'You're now living in the biggest fire break in Victoria. You'll be the safest place going' is a common comment. But who knows whether the wind won't come from a different direction and hit what wasn't burnt last time, or that grass fires—rather than tall timbers flinging fatal fireballs—won't be the threat? There are no safe assumptions.

It will be at least two more seasons before our new house is built and we face endless bureaucratic hurdling just to get the proper pieces of paper. We are among the lucky ones, though, not having to rush into house-building to restore a roof over our heads. Members of services clubs who have been helping those still relying on temporary accommodation—families crammed under canvas or in tents, caravans or converted portable classrooms—expressed grave concern that some were in danger of making hasty decisions that would lead to major disappointments and costly repairs down the track. Psychologically, the breathing space between temporary living and permanent housing has been vital for us and our extended family and friends.

By mid-December, our case manager Bernadette had finished her secondment and the case-worker team was being wound up. Many survivors felt it was too soon to be without this backup, but the thinking behind it was that from then on most issues would be about building and to this end building advisory services were put in place. Again, only time will tell whether people suffer because of this.

But human beings are resilient and self-help groups are emerging, the community's say growing stronger as previously disparate groupings find a new common goal and voice. The mountain houses a phenomenal range of skills which, if harnessed, can ensure the community thrives. One such collective developed among people who were building or rebuilding, to exchange information, source best-priced materials, and volunteer or request labour when needed. There was no formal arrangement, no government backing, no politics—just stalwart, practical people sharing an experience.

While all that has been happening on the outside, life in the barn has taken shape too. There are now numerous mornings when I try not to make a racket and disturb the bundle blissfully asleep on the sofa bed. There's just a hint of hair showing from under the doona, but otherwise no movement. She'll have to get a shake soon, though, in time for the trip down the hill either with me on the way to work or later, and more leisurely, with Sean. It is a welcome return to normality, to again be hearing Carissa's appeal, 'Can I hook up with you guys tonight?' For seven months, while we were living with others and she had to work through what she'd experienced, that couldn't happen.

It was within weeks of our moving into the barn that our regular house guest felt the need to be back, and two jaded fire survivors couldn't have been happier. She hasn't batted an eyelid about the building clutter, the lack of dedicated personal space or the fact that we had to continue using the portaloo for several months because the indoor plumbing took longer than expected. I recall as a small child being surprised to discover some relatives had an outside toilet that demanded a torch and more than a little courage when a night trip was required. Here we are three generations later, with a parallel memory in the making.

As Christmas loomed, our 'tribe' was bearing some resemblance to its old self. Harley had been home for several months and had grooved back into his old routine, periodically sneaking off to visit properties that are no longer there. Tania missed him so much after he'd gone that we adopted a new little refugee for her from the RSPCA. Meg gets a little slower every month; Jazz continues to dominate all and invade the bed. Ricky has a new best buddy: as there could be no replacement for Eliza, we opted for the opposite end of the spectrum, in the form of Cinnamon, a miniature horse also garnered from the RSPCA.

King parrots and eastern rosellas are once again perching on branches, some of them cheeky enough to eat out of your hand. The owls are back hooting at night; the lyrebirds have returned in fine voice too. Echidnas paddle through the gravel on the roadsides and a large kangaroo has taken to bounding through our paddock in the mornings. By next summer we hope to have planted enough shrubs to attract the honeyeaters and butterflies. We won't have time to organise a full and productive vegie garden this year, but it will rise again. Our chickens fell victim to hungry foxes and won't be replaced until a new, safe run can be built.

So, life and the seasons go on. The paddocks are browning off quickly and summer promises to be an extended stinker; we will deal with it as it occurs. To our joy, our shady sycamore tree sprang back into leafy life, with a few holes in the canopy but otherwise alive and well. The large ash at the back of the house was pronounced moribund, though, and had to be removed, bequeathing us a veritable mountain of potential firewood. With great trepidation, we asked an arborist to give us his expert opinion on the massive ash at the front, whose top crashed onto Deviation Road the night of the fires; its huge base had smouldered for days.

'It's a fabulous tree. A few dead branches off here and there and it will be there for a long time yet,' declared the arborist. 'And if something does make it fall, it won't land where the new house is going be.' We were inexpressably relieved that this giant had seen off everything mother nature had thrown at it so far, and will continue to provide habitat for all those birds and animals.

John and Julie drop in regularly to check out the barn's progress, bring over a plant or have a chat, and often stay for an impromptu meal. We do the same in reverse. The four of us have been bound even more closely by the enormity of our shared experience—on Black Saturday, and thereafter.

There are still days when the loss and sadness are overwhelming, when the task ahead seems just too daunting, but these feelings pass a little more quickly now. Our small part of the world has turned green again: the eucalypt and wattle seeds have sprung into baby trees, the pastures are lush, and summer-flowering perennials have pushed through the soil. The human damage is likely to take a lot longer to heal, though.

We continue to deal with newly reordered priorities, examining what is really valuable to us. We view the gift of life through different eyes, knowing that within the space of hours everything we love can be destroyed. A year after Black Saturday the cost will again be counted, but the raw statistics don't quite convey the true picture of the 400 individual fires that raged in Victoria in February 2009, the 173 people who died, the 2000 or more houses destroyed and damaged, the 7000 people left homeless. Behind each of those figures is an extended circle of family and friends, not to mention the many people involved in recovery efforts. The young man who came to expertly fell our dead trees summed it up when he recounted his journey into the fire zone the day after Black Saturday, helping to remove the dangerous roadside flora that was hampering efforts to get emergency crews in. Even now he remembers the powerful shock of the death and destruction he faced, and how he had to steel himself for each subsequent visit. The same goes for the many soldiers, police officers, ambulance crews, firefighters, doctors, counsellors and aid-agency workers who endured not only horrific scenes during the fires but also subsequent, ongoing human tragedy.

Our story is only one of many, but if in the telling it gives some hope or direction to others battling through the recovery process, or inspires even one family to seriously discuss and plan the best way to stay safe when we again face conditions that may engender the 'perfect storm', then some good will have come from that fateful day. The expression 'It can never happen to me' has left our vocabulary for good. What the future holds, none of us can predict. But at least we have one, unlike 173 others.

Acknowledgements

WHEN the worst day of our lives occurred on 7 February 2009, my immediate family were reliant on the phenomenal efforts provided by a range of emergency services. The police, ambulance crews, firefighters, army personnel and recovery workers, who risked their own safety to enter our devastated and shocked communities, cared for us with such kindness and professionalism. Thank you to all of you.

I would also like to thank our neighbours Julie Hansen and John Christadoulou, who overcame their own fears to provide us with a safe haven and a temporary home, and who continue to support us in so many precious ways.

A special thanks to the RSPCA for relieving the stress over our much loved animals, and for their wonderful ongoing efforts.

But, most of all, this book is for the families of the 173 people who so tragically lost the battle that day, for the injured, for the thousands whose lives have changed forever, and for the communities who still have such a long and difficult journey of recovery ahead of them.